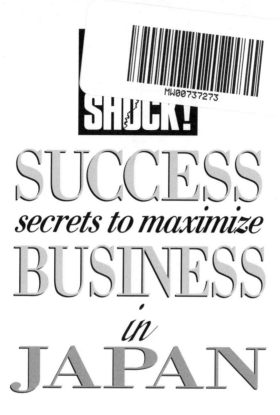

SHOCK!

SUCCESS
secrets to maximize
BUSINESS
in
JAPAN

Carin Holroyd & Ken Coates

Graphic Arts Center Publishing Company
Portland, Oregon

All photographs by Ken Coates

© 1999, 2000 Times Media Private Limited

This book is published by special
arrangement with Times Media Private Limited
A member of the Times Publishing Group
Times Centre, 1 New Industrial Road, Singapore 536196
International Standard Book Number 1-55868-480-8
Library of Congress Catalog Number 99-65081
Graphic Arts Center Publishing Company
P.O. Box 10306 • Portland Oregon 97296-0306 • (503)226-2402

Printed in Singapore

Contents

Introduction

This book began in the most "Japanese" fashion. One of Carin's old friends had learned, through another friend, that a company in Asia was looking for someone to write a book on doing business in Japan. We got in contact with the friend of a friend and, with his gracious assistance, made contact with Times Editions of Singapore. We are particularly grateful to Mae Sagar and Peter Needham for providing this initial connection and for, therefore, making this book possible.

A great deal has been written about the Japanese economy and Japanese business in recent years, and newcomers to the country might well be baffled by the diversity of opinion about Japan. We come to this work from very different directions. Carin is a longtime Japan "hand." She speaks the language, has lived in the country for, collectively, several years, and most recently spent three months in Tokyo studying North American business adaptations to the Japanese market. She is a specialist in the area of Japanese business and international trade. I, on the other hand, am one of those "typical" foreigners who was more than a little intimidated by Japan and the prospect of being lost amidst millions of non-English speaking Japanese. My first visit to Japan in 1996 transformed my image of the country, and I now eagerly await each and every opportunity to return to it. What follows seeks to bring both of our perspectives—the specialist and the newcomer— to bear on questions of the greatest concern to business people wishing to enter the Japanese market.

The book is roughly divided into two sections. In the first, we cover the generalities of the Japanese situation and provide an overview of the country's economic history, contemporary national economy, and business environment. In the second section, we turn to more pragmatic details and consider the ways in which foreign business people, new to the Japanese market, might best prepare themselves for the opportunities. Japan is not an easy place to do business, but it holds considerable promise for those determined enough and creative enough to take up the challenge. We are both unabashed in our affection for the country and its people, and hope that our enthusiasm (and our cautions) come through in the pages that follow.

Good luck on your business trip to Japan! We trust that you will find your encounter with the country to be as personally and professionally rewarding as we have found our Japanese experiences. We hope, finally, that this book will make you more enthusiastic about the prospects of succeeding in business in Japan, and that the pages will provide guidance, insight, suggestions, and warnings that will help you in your business dealings with the country.

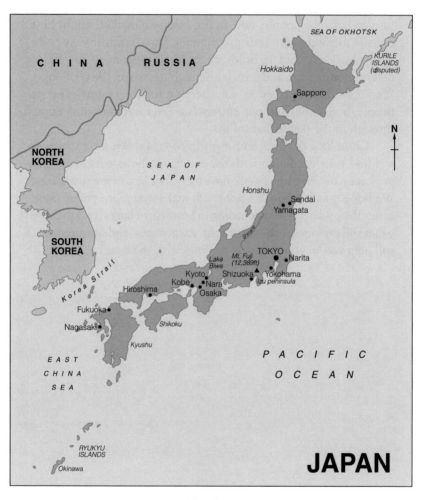

Map of Japan

CHAPTER 1

That Special Place Called Nippon

The second half of the 1990s has not been particularly kind to the Japanese economy—or so it seems from a distance. The country has endured a series of major problems, capped by the spectacular collapse of several major financial institutions in late 1997. The real estate boom that fueled Japan's "bubble economy" slipped dramatically, particularly in Tokyo. Major national investments in artificial intelligence, high-definition television, and other technology-based innovations appear to have produced few results. Ten years ago, the Japanese were buying up major art collections, prime pieces of American real estate, and seemed to be purchasing resources and companies in every corner of the globe. More recently, the news is full of stories of Japanese sell-offs of overseas investments, reductions in international exposure, and unusually high rates of bankruptcy and unemployment rates on the domestic scene. A decade ago, the goal seemed to be to jump onto the Japanese juggernaut before all profitable opportunities disappeared; now, the task seems to be to navigate through the morass of financial chaos and uncertainty and to find commercial openings in an environment of fading dreams and diminished expectations.

Most outsiders misunderstood Japan's aspirations during the 1980s boom, and they continue to overstate the nature and extent of the current difficulties. That they do so illustrates the continuing challenge that foreigners face when attempting to understand Japan and to determine the best way of doing business in the land of the rising sun. On the one hand, Westerners (particularly North Americans) overestimate the uniqueness of Japan. Comparing

Japan to the United States or Canada produces a variety of statistical indices of sharp distinctions and unusual differences; extending the comparisons to a more global review illustrates that Japan is not as unusual as popular wisdom would have it. At the same time, however, outsiders rarely take the time to understand the historical and cultural roots of Japanese society and, therefore, of Japanese commerce. As a consequence, they often make significant mistakes in interpreting and anticipating Japanese business situations.

The goal of this book is simple—to provide business people with a basic introduction to Japan and to offer those interested in entering this dynamic and complicated commercial world a guide to the intricacies of Japanese business. No single volume, however insightful and creative, can provide readers with sufficient depth or detail to overcome the need for hands-on experience. We hope that this book will make the initial business and professional encounters as successful as possible and that readers will be encouraged to understand the people and business culture of this fascinating country.

The Mystique of Japan

Japan baffles most newcomers. It is not that the country is overly crowded—China or Indonesia provide far more graphic evidence of the "crush of humanity" in Asia. It is not that Tokyo, most new arrivals' first point of entry into the country, is particularly congested, chaotic, or imposing—Bangkok or Manila are far more complicated and difficult to figure out. It is not even that the country is particularly capitalistic or frenetic—the prize in these categories would likely go to Hong Kong or Singapore. It is not, surprisingly, that the country is particularly "Asian" in outlook or presence—Japan is the most Westernized of Asian nations and, language aside, can look and feel familiar to a Westerner.

Perhaps Japan surprises most outsiders simply because of its success. The islands of the Japanese archipelago are not richly

Rice fields abound in Niigata prefecture.

endowed in natural resources, and the hundreds of islands and mountains that make up the country do not lend themselves well to agricultural development. But, this is home to the world's second largest economy—fully 80% of the size of the US economy, with only 126 million Japanese to the 300 million Americans—and to one of the most sophisticated societies, both in terms of technology and commercial activity.

Japan is also host to a strikingly traditional society, with women in *kimonos* walking side by side with power-dressing female executives, and with a tightly protected agrarian community living in a nation that operates over 60% of the world's industrial robots. This is a land of immense contradictions, of tradition and modernity, of a desire to hold onto the past and a willingness to lead the way into the future. Japan includes the urban complexity of Tokyo and the rural isolation of Niigata prefecture. It is the country that has bestowed the haunting beauty of *haiku* and, to much of the world, remains the unrepentant aggressor of World War II. Japan is the nation that popularized such concepts as "just in time" manufacturing; yet, the country holds on (less tightly now that in the past) to lifetime employment structures in its larger corporations.

These internal tensions are the essence of Japan, not the exceptions. For Japan is a nation that looks to a rich history and toward an uncertain future simultaneously. Despite the seeming contradictions, and perhaps because of them, Japan succeeds. The nation has an extremely strong work ethic; a willingness to subordinate personal goals to those of the company, the community, and the nation; and a remarkable track record for innovation. It is a country that has reinvented itself several times in the past century, not always with pleasant results, and is mindful of the need to prepare itself for the significant challenges that lie ahead in the twenty-first century.

For generations, the Japanese separated themselves from the rest of the world, creating a cloud of misunderstanding that is only now starting to lift. Historically, complications of language and culture have made it difficult for outsiders to comprehend the "Japanese mind," further enhancing the Japanese mystique.

Lifting the Veil
Business people cannot afford to ignore Japan. Both the remarkable surge of the 1980s and the downturn of the late 1990s demonstrated the folly of failing to keep abreast of developments in the Japanese economy. And Japan continues to position itself as a major player in the global economy, particularly through its determination to retain a leadership role in the development and implementation of new technologies. Japan offers a rich, dynamic, and outward-looking consumer market—one of the most intriguing consumer cultures in the world. The business community likewise continues to search for opportunities to innovate and to expand its international presence. And, due to recent changes in domestic

Japan at a Glance

It is important to keep Japan in perspective, to ensure that you do not underestimate or overestimate the country. Here are some useful basic details about the country:

Size 378,000 sq. km, slightly smaller than the State of California.

Islands Japan consists of four major islands—Hokkaido, Honshu, Shikoku, and Kyushu. In total, there are some 3,000 occupied islands in the country.

Japanese Landscape Approximately 11% of Japan's land mass is suitable for agriculture. Much of the rest consists of rugged, mountainous terrain.

Climate Japan generally enjoys a temperate climate, characterized by hot and humid summers and cool winters. The main islands of Honshu and Kyushu get only occasional dustings of snow at the lower elevations, but the mountainous regions get hit with heavy snowfalls throughout the winter. Hokkaido, to the north, experiences relatively severe winters and is noted for its winter recreational activities. Conversely, Okinawa in the far south has a near-tropical climate and is quite warm all year round.

Warnings Japan is subject to frequent earthquakes (close to 1,500 a year, but very few of the magnitude of the Kobe earthquake of 1995). Also, the country has numerous volcanoes (the vast majority inactive) and is vulnerable to *tsunamis*, or tidal waves.

Population 125.7 million (1997 estimate). Of this population, 16% is over 65 years of age. This is one of the highest percentages of senior citizens of any country in the world. The life expectancy of over 80 years is, likewise, one of the highest.

Population Change Japan has low birth and death rates. It also experiences a slight net population loss through immigration. In recent years, efforts have been made to attract Japanese Brazilians and others of Japanese ancestry living outside Japan back to the country to offset the stagnating growth rate.

Religion While most Japanese do not consider themselves to be religious, 84% of the people observe both Shinto and Buddhist faiths, although typically in a very informal fashion. The 16% of the population that practices other religions includes a small Christian population.

Administrative Structure Japan operates through a strong, centralized government, with 47 prefectures providing local administration. The prefectures are Aichi, Akita, Aomori, Chiba, Ehime, Fukui, Fukuoka, Fukushima, Gifu, Gumma, Hiroshima, Hokkaido, Hyogo, Ibaraki, Ishikawa, Iwate, Kagawa, Kagoshima, Kanagawa, Kochi, Kumamoto, Kyoto, Mie, Miyagi, Miyazaki, Nagano, Nagasaki, Nara, Niigata, Oita, Okayama, Okinawa, Osaka, Saga, Saitama, Shiga, Shimane, Shizuoka, Tochigi, Tokushima, Tokyo, Tottori, Toyama, Wakayama, Yamagata, Yamaguchi, and Yamanashi.

Regional Economies Outsiders tend to see Japan as a single, highly industrialized, and strong Westernized economy. This image is misleading. The corridor from Tokyo to Osaka fits this description, and the area around other major centuries, such as Hiroshima, is typically heavily developed. But the outlying districts tend to be more agricultural and, often, considerably poorer. The extreme case is the Ryukyu Islands (more commonly known as Okinawa), an area that suffers from considerable economic hardship. The emphasis placed by foreign business people on the Tokyo megalopolis means that important commercial opportunities are missed in the outlying areas. The economy of the Sendai region north of Tokyo, for example, is roughly the same size as that of Australian economy.

regulations and government policies regarding foreign ownership, Japan is increasingly open to external investment and involvement, although the proportion of its economic base owned by foreigners is small by international standards. Successful business operations in Japan, however, require that the veil of mysticism and misunderstanding be lifted. Foreign business people will have to understand the reality of Japanese society and culture, and recognize the complexities of the Japanese business environment. To do so requires, first and foremost, a willingness to move beyond stereotypes and fixed assumptions and to take a new look at Japan and the Japanese.

Generations of Isolation

It is impossible to understand a country without knowing a little about its history, and this is never more the case than with Japan. It is an ancient society with roots that lie several thousand years deep in the soil of the archipelago. The islands had a small number of indigenous peoples, most notably the Ainu, but these societies were gradually pushed to the north as newcomers arrived from Korea. Their location several hundred miles from the coast of China and Korea provided a strong measure of protection from other peoples, and protected Japan from several waves of conquest that overran the nearby continent. Japan developed with a great degree of isolation, close enough to trade and to exchange ideas and cultural elements with the continent, but sufficiently far away to evolve largely on its own terms.

When the first Europeans (Jesuit missionaries and Portuguese traders) ventured into the area in the sixteenth century, the Japanese were determined to keep the foreigners at bay. (In most places around the world, newcomers were welcomed and trade and other contacts developed. Over time, this led most of the Asian societies, with the exception of Thailand, into European imperial domination. The rulers of Japan would have none of this.) By the early 1600s, foreign traders were restricted to a single trading post near Nagasaki. Missionaries, often the vanguard of European control, were initially tolerated but then expelled. The Japanese were ordered to have no contact with the outside world. While other Asian societies, for better or worse, found themselves gradually affected by the economic, religious, social, and political influences from Europe, the Japanese were steadfast in their determination to stay aloof and to protect their islands for their own use.

Japan enjoyed over 250 years of self-imposed isolation, at a time when many other non-European societies were experiencing the effects of colonization and external domination. This period was one of general peace and harmony throughout Japan, and saw the establishment of many of the cultural and social foundations that are now associated with the country and society. Standing apart from the world encouraged the development of a relatively harmonious and highly homogeneous Japanese society. It also meant that, in commercial and technological terms, the Japanese remained out of step with a world that was experiencing rapid developments in manufacturing, transportation, and science and technology.

Japan's splendid and self-imposed isolation ended in the mid-nineteenth century. Increasingly, aggressive foreign interests led by the United States made clear their determination to enter Japan, by force if necessary. More than 250 years of Japanese isolation stood at risk. Realizing that the mighty Americans, with Commodore Perry's "Black" ships at the forefront, had the military power to enforce their will, Japan's rulers took decisive action. They threw open their lands to the intruders, who found the barriers of language and culture to be sufficiently formidable as to retard their advance, and then went on the offensive. They reasoned that if Japan was to be forced to become a member of the world community, it should do so quickly and with enthusiasm. Students and officials were dispatched to the United States, England, and Europe to learn about the Western industrial "miracle." Major Western texts were translated into Japanese. And the advances of the industrialized world—railways, factories, and urban developments—were quickly mirrored in Japan.

This era is know as the Meiji Revolution, one of the most remarkable national transformations in the history of the world. The Japan of the mid-nineteenth century was agrarian, feudal, non-industrial, and incredibly insular and isolated. The Japan of the first years of the twentieth century, a mere 50 years later, was rapidly industrializing, increasingly urban, much more democratic, better educated, and reasonably well-connected to the rest of the world. Japanese students and officials studied abroad; Western dress and lifestyle were imitated in Japan. Industrial expansion created a new class of wealthy entrepreneurs, who discovered that the new order honored business leaders in a way that the old Tokogawa system did not. In just over two generations, Japan remade itself from inside out, and went from being one of the most isolated societies in Asia to the most Westernized. In the process, the country demonstrated a capacity for innovation, creativity, national leadership, and communal sacrifice that was virtually unmatched.

Japan's Emergence as a World Power

Japan's rapid industrialization launched the country onto the world stage. The tremendous expansion of factory production, railways, and cities created new pockets of wealth—little of which passed into the hands of the working class. Japanese authorities used the new prosperity to continue the process of nation-building and to tie the disparate peoples of the archipelago into a coherent national whole. The creation of a nationwide education system and democratic institutions gave residents a greater role in the governing of the country. But the Japanese had grander visions, which were rooted in their encounter with Western nation states, particularly the United States and the imperial powers that, at the turn of the century, still governed much of the world. Revealing a talent for imitation and innovation, which had rarely before been seen, the Japanese modeled their new country on the successful examples of the United States, Britain, and then West Germany.

From these countries, the Japanese learned the fundamental importance of military power—already deeply embedded in the Japanese value system—and of establishing an international presence. Japan expanded its army and navy, and, at a time when most of the world remained under imperial control, asserted its independence and desire for respect on the international stage. It earned its desired status early in the twentieth century. In the years 1894 and 1895, Japan battled with China for control of Korea and, to the surprise of many, defeated the much larger nation. Japan went to war against Russia in 1904 and, much to the shock of European onlookers, became the first non-European power in centuries to emerge victorious. Japan subsequently capitalized on this victory to assume control of part of Manchuria and, in 1910, to assume full control of the Korean Peninsula. (The occupation, still remembered unfavorably by the Koreans after several generations, gave Japan a foothold on the continent.) At a time when European powers exerted colonial dominance over much of the earth, Japan had emerged as a formidable rival.

After Russia's capitulation in 1905, Japan assumed that it would gain new respect among the world community and become the first Asian population to operate on equal terms with the imperialist powers of Europe. And it did so, figuring quite prominently in the early workings of the post-World War I League of Nations. The country continued to industrialize, built up an even larger military, and began to cast covetous eyes on the surrounding lands. In the 1930s, the Japanese moved toward China, launching an armed invasion that involved a vicious and determined assault on the city of Nanking. By the late 1930s, as European and other Western powers worried about the threat of Nazi Germany, the Japanese solidified their hold on Korea and parts of China. They also planned for an even more daring assault.

Japan's expansionist policy had inherent difficulties, for the country had quickly outgrown its resource base and become increasingly reliant on supplies imported from other lands. Given Japan's astonishing economic performance, it is not surprising that its leaders would begin to look at less developed territories in Korea, China, and Southeast Asia. While the Japanese attempted to portray their growing ambition for international expansion as an attempt to develop an East Asian Co-Prosperity Sphere, other nations were less impressed with the growing signs of Japanese aggression.

The Pacific War began in earnest when the Japanese made their way to North Vietnam in the summer of 1940. Japan followed up with its strike on Pearl Harbor, Hawaii. Japanese history books have long portrayed this surprise attack as a pre-emptive strike, designed to protect Japan from an anticipated American assault, a different story altogether from the one told in Western texts. With lightening quickness, they expanded their attacks. The Japanese advance continued with an attack on the British stronghold of Hong Kong. British and Allied soldiers held out for a short while, but they were quickly overrun by the larger and better armed Japanese troops. They kept going, pushing the Americans out of the Philippines, tossing the British out of Singapore, brushing aside the Dutch in Indonesia, and moving steadily through the tropical islands of the South Pacific. The Japanese expansion included small invasions of the Aleutian Islands in Alaska, the bombing of Darwin, Australia, and attacks throughout Southeast Asia. At the height of Japanese domination, the country controlled vast tracts of land throughout Asia; the dream of regional domination appeared to have become a reality.

The rest of the story is well known. The Allied powers, principally the United States, recovered from the shock of the initial attacks. They moved, through a series of pivotal naval battles and island-hopping across the South Pacific, to push the Japanese back into their national stronghold. Japan fought on, driven by the love of nation and Emperor, and by the belief in its own invincibility. But the Allies outnumbered the Japanese troops and brought vast resources to bear on what was increasingly shown to be an isolated island bastion. Mass bombings of major cities and industrial establishments took their toll, both in terms of human lives and material costs, but the Japanese persisted. Even the successful American invasion of Okinawa, marked by a frenetic defense by the local population and one of the most bitter battles of this or any war, did not convince the Japanese that the war was over.

The end came with surprising quickness. The American population prepared itself for a costly and time-consuming invasion of the main Japanese islands. The Japanese dug themselves in for a protracted and determined defense of their homeland. The preparations proved unnecessary. On August 6, 1945, the United States dropped an atomic bomb on Hiroshima. Three days later, they dropped a second bomb on Nagasaki. Endless debate has followed the rationale behind the American decision to use this ultimate weapon. The atomic explosions rocked Japan to its core. Emperor Hirohito was convinced that Japan had to surrender, and the voices demanding that the country fight to the end were ultimately ignored. Emperor Hirohito took the remarkable step of appearing on national radio—no Japanese commoner had so much as heard his voice before this pronouncement—to announce that Japan had surrendered. World War II was over.

The loss marked a bitter turning point for Japan. Dreams of territorial conquest and political domination on a scale long enjoyed by the major European powers had vanished. The idea of an East Asian Co-Prosperity Sphere—led, naturally enough, by the Japanese—was dead. Japan had, instead, earned the enmity of most of its neighbors, who would long remember the acts of military brutality and the legacy of armed occupation that accompanied the Japanese expansion. World War II was, in many ways, a turning point for Japan, for it gave the lie to the argument that the country could and should establish regional and international dominance through territorial conquest and acquisition. It also provided strong evidence that Japan was a formidable foe, much stronger, more creative, and more determined than Western observers had ever assumed.

The Legacy of World War II

The end of World War II left Japan battered almost beyond belief. For a start, there was the physical damage to the country. Tokyo lay in smoldering ruins. Major cities, Hiroshima and Nagasaki among them, had been destroyed by the relentless pounding of Allied bombers. The nation had lost much of an entire generation of young men, causalities of a decade-long struggle for territorial expansion. The economy lay in tatters so much so that the specter of mass starvation hung over Japan in the first years following the war.

To make things worse, the country remained occupied, nominally by an Allied force but, in reality, by the United States. Led by General Douglas McArthur, the Americans imposed a new economic order on the country and attempted to break up the *zaibatsu,* or business conglomerates, that had dominated the country before the war. They imposed a new constitution, drafted by a small group of Americans, on the country. Among other elements, the constitution forbade Japan from re-establishing a regular army. Although Japan had had considerable experience with parliamentary democracy before the war, the American-imposed system also established a constitutional foundation for democratic governance.

Japan had been thoroughly and resoundingly thrashed during the World War II. The people warmed quickly to the relative gentleness of the American occupation, for the leaders had warned them to expect far worse from the Yankee soldiers. And, as did the Germans in Europe, they benefited from the American and Allied decision not to punish the vanquished in the post-war period, although most of the former leaders were imprisoned, punished, or banned from having an active presence in Japanese society.

For most Japanese, the five-year American occupation was generally benign, and many of the sweeping social and political reforms were widely applauded. Assistance was provided directly to people in need of food and shelter, and to companies seeking to re-establish their operations. The generosity was rooted in the realization that post-World War I mean-spiritedness was an underlying cause of the rise of the Nazis in Germany. And, in the rapidly unfolding reality of the Cold War, the Americans wanted to ensure that their former enemies did not transfer into the Soviet camp. The peace then proved to be less demoralizing than anticipated by the Japanese, and they looked for ways to rebuild their country and society.

Even with these developments, few expected the Japanese to rebound quickly from the debacle and devastation of World War II. The war represented the most assertive statement of the Japanese nation, and as a consequence, the defeat indicated a profound repudiation of the country's aspirations. It was clear, too, that the Americans expected Japan to develop within clear parameters—a respect for democratic structures, limited government control over the economy, strong support for anti-Communist forces, and greater attention to American-style civil rights. Logic and history suggested that it would take some time for the Japanese to overcome the physical legacy of the war and to cope with the psychological and emotional pain of loss, occupation, and external control.

Rebuilding the Country

But as the Japanese had done during the Meiji era, they rallied and quickly rebounded. The industrial structure, aided in no small measure by the American financial support, was quickly rebuilt. The same commitment to nation that fueled the Japanese support for the war effort now went into rebuilding the country. Individuals and families placed on hold their personal expectations and ambitions in order that Japan could quickly re-establish itself as an influential economic and political power. Far from wallowing in the devastation of war, the Japanese seemed to find determination in their situation. Within 15 years, and mirroring a process of national rebuilding undertaken in West Germany, Japan had overcome the legacy of World War II. Although the country remained considerably behind the West in per capita income, and although Japan had, by the 1960s, become synonymous with mediocre, cheap merchandise, the nation had provided its people with an industrial base and with reasons to be optimistic about the future.

The Excesses of War

The war left other legacies, some of which remain in play to the present. Japanese forces in Asia during World War II engaged in acts of striking brutality, even by normal military standards. The "rape" of Nanking (December 1937–January 1938) remains a bitter memory for many Chinese. Even more importantly, various indignities inflicted upon the Korean people are widely and angrily remembered. During the war, the Japanese forced hundreds of Korean women to serve as prostitutes, whom they called "comfort women," for Japanese troops. Only in 1998 did Japan finally began to apologize to and compensate these women for the wartime abuse.

Similar situations hold in many quarters. British and Canadians troops have not forgotten the Japanese attack on Hong Kong; the survivors passed years in intolerable conditions in Japanese prisoner of war camps. Anger toward the Japanese occupying forces continues to condition responses to the country in Singapore, the Philippines, Indonesia, New Zealand, and Australia, as well as throughout the South Pacific. Time has healed some wounds, but the refusal by the Japanese to acknowledge the excesses of World War II has ensured that some continue to fester.

23

This is true also of relations between the United States and Japan. The post-war period saw the development of US-Japan trade into one of the world's most important and extensive trading relationships. (It is the second largest in the world, falling behind only US-Canada trade.) On the surface, all appears well. But lingering beneath this impressive and important trading relationship is the long-standing legacy of mistrust and misunderstanding. During World War II, racial stereotypes and hostilities developed on both sides of the battlefield. The Americans typically saw the Japanese as barbaric, inhumane, and vicious; it might well surprise them to discover that the Japanese had a similar impression of the American soldiers. That these images were created, in large measure, out of wartime propaganda does not diminish their fundamental importance to US-Japan relations.

The end of the war also killed Japanese aspirations for territorial expansion. Although the idea of a Japan-dominated regime in East Asia appealed greatly to Japanese leaders, their attempted implementation of the strategy failed. The elimination of the territorial imperative, however, did not end Japan's need for resources and markets in other lands or their expectation that they could and should provide leadership for the region. Japan could not thrive without access to raw materials and, equally, without markets for its products. The country was, by definition, a trading nation. Its future prosperity rested substantially on its ability to re-establish trading connections, as well as rebuild its industrial and financial systems, and business networks. Efforts to do so ran up against widespread anger and hostility over World War II; the Asian and Western sides would not soon forget Japan's role in the world's greatest military conflict.

The Re-emergence of Japan

Few visitors to Japan in the late 1940s would have been so bold as to forecast the country's emergence as an economic superpower.

Optimists hoped that the nation would rebuild and that the country could return to economic self-sufficiency. The vindictive—and there were many—hoped that Japan would wallow in poverty and despair for decades. The Japanese appeared to be contrite about the war; there was no post-war militarism or hyped-up nationalism to suggest that the people wanted to re-establish past glories. Instead, the nation accepted the dictates of the occupying powers, principally the United States, and endured the many public humiliations that attended military conquest. (Perhaps the most significant of the many admissions required of the Japanese was the declaration that Emperor Hirohito was not "God" and to the rendering of his role as purely symbolic.)

With a determination that was shared by the similarly war-ravaged Germans, the Japanese turned their attention to rebuilding their industrial base. American efforts to destroy and replace the zaibatsu proved generally unsuccessful. These leading industrial conglomerates overcame the administrative and legal restrictions placed on them by the occupying powers and re-established themselves at the core of the Japanese economy.

Phenomenal Growth

Freed from the costs of maintaining an active army—the United States provided the military protection required during the Cold War—the government of Japan turned its attention to economic growth. It was aided, in the short term, by the onset of the Korean War, which provided a spark for Japanese industrial production. Led by the Ministry of International Trade and Industry (MITI) and the Ministry of Finance (MOF), and spurred on by the country's ability to attract the best and brightest into the ranks of the civil service, the government launched a state-orchestrated strategy for industrial expansion. This effort was capped, in the 1960s, by Prime Minister Ikeda's bold promise that the country would double personal incomes within 10 years. He was wrong. The nation's economy and prosperity grew faster than had been forecast.

Japan's accelerated economic growth rested on the step-wise move through several key transitions. In the 1950s and 1960s, the country capitalized on a cheap labor force and made significant inroads into international markets for textiles and low-cost items. The phrase "Made in Japan" became synonymous with cheap, poorly produced trinkets and curiosity items. While hardly the base for world economic prominence, this strategy put the nation's workers back into the factories and stimulated considerable internal development. By the 1960s, the Japanese had shifted their attention to heavy industry and, paying little heed to the long-term environmental consequences of their investments, made massive expenditures on steel-making, shipbuilding, and other major industrial operations. A commitment to high quality products and reliability in delivery ensured that the Japanese companies found sizable world markets for their products.

From Portable Radios to Cars

The Japanese also moved into other fields. The nation's electronic manufacturers were among the first to recognize the commercial importance of transistorization. Firms, such as Sony and Hitachi, capitalized on the development of miniature electronic components and produced the first wave of portable radios. Despite its image as a stodgy, conservative, cultural backwater, Japan was making some of the most important items of the 1960s consumer revolution.

Around this time, Japanese auto makers sent their first shiploads of small, inexpensive commuter cars to North America. These vehicles, already popular on the congested roads of Asia, were mocked by North American car manufacturers, who remained convinced that their larger, more powerful machines would hold onto their historic market share. They were wrong, although it took a decade for companies such as Toyota, Datsun (now Nissan) and Mazda to establish credibility in the vital United States market. Japan had, by the late 1960s, overcome the miseries of World War II and had completed a remarkable economic "miracle."

The early 1970s seemed to threaten the hard-won prosperity. The oil shocks of 1973 and 1978 appeared to knock the underpinnings from the Japanese industrial machine. Japan had virtually no domestic energy supplies and relied almost entirely on imported oil. The dramatic price increases for oil cut a huge swath through Japanese corporate profits. Western observers, at a loss to explain the country's dramatic turnaround, anticipated that the oil crisis would bring Japan to its knees. But the country responded, imposing conservation measures (while, at the same time, cleaning up some of the most serious environmental problems), re-jigging industrial practices to ensure efficiency, and shifting into less energy-intensive industries. The transition, conducted with remarkable speed, worked, and Japan emerged from the chaos of the oil crisis with an invigorated and refocused industrial plant.

Japanese business had, to put it simply, re-invented itself once again. A spate of new industrial innovations, including robotics (Japan is the world's largest producer and user of industrial robots) and "just-in-time" manufacturing and retailing operations, created new opportunities and advantages for Japanese firms. While many Western nations experienced greater strife between labor and management during the inflationary years of the 1970s and early 1980s, Japan's more cooperative model of labor relations ensured industrial peace and worker assistance in company re-organizations.* Japan, often derided as a nation of imitators lacking in creativity, made enormous and timely investments in the emerging fields of computers and electronic components.

* Japan has not always enjoyed harmonious relations between workers and management. Several times in the 1950s and 1960s, dramatic and even violent strikes had worried several of the country's major employers. By the late 1960s, however, the system had evolved into its current style.

Surge in Foreign Direct Investment

The determination to carve out important and lasting market niches in high-technology areas proved prescient. By the mid-1980s, Japan had developed considerable dominance in key industrial fields, including automobile manufacturing, computer components, electrical supplies, and super-conductors and related products. The nation had, as well, emerged as the world's second largest economy, no small feat given its limited national resources. A raging real estate market, particularly in Tokyo, made Japanese companies land and asset rich, and this combined with a desire to avoid a protectionist backlash against Japan's ballooning trade surpluses, fueled a foreign direct investment frenzy that sparked considerable hostility in the United States, Australia, and New Zealand.

In the late 1990s, Japanese firms again began to invest heavily overseas. This time, the bulk of the manufacturing investment shifted to low-wage countries, principally in Southeast Asia, preserving the high-wage, knowledge intensive processes for Japanese workers. Japan was now firmly entrenched as a world economic power so much so that xenophobic reactions to Japanese investment became quite commonplace. This, however, was an inevitable price for success, for Japanese firms and the government of Japan realized that their country's economic future lay in foreign trade and overseas investments.

A Hard Nut to Crack

What particularly annoyed international competitors and foreign governments was the relative impenetrability of the Japanese market. While Japanese firms were enthusiastic about investing outside the country—buying up large portions of the Hawaiian and Australian Gold Coast hotel stock for example—and selling their products around the world, non-Japanese companies seeking to enter the Japanese market found their way stalled by a maze of regulations, restrictions, and cultural barriers. American auto makers, for example, complained about their inability to penetrate

The bridge at Nikko is a popular Japanese tourist site.

the Japanese consumer market. (They might have done better had they produced cars that suited Japanese tastes and driving conditions!) Although it was possible to do business in Japan— primarily for those selling raw materials—companies seeking to market consumer products typically faced considerable difficulty. They were dissuaded from trying, often times, by the complexity of the distribution system and the intricacies of Japanese culture, which Japanese officials and companies often utilized to keep competitors at bay.

After the 1985 Plaza Accord, which mandated a sharp rise in the value of the yen, Japanese companies focused their marketing attentions outside their country. They sought, in particular, to address consumer needs in the United States. New products were designed for and tested in the United States first; if and when they proved successful, they were later released for domestic consumption. The goal, driven by the nation's reliance on international trade, was to maintain a sizable presence in Western markets. The rising value of the yen, which outsiders again erroneously predicted would bring Japan to its economic knees, forced a reorientation of national economic priorities. Greater value was now attached to producing goods for the local market; Japan became the test-bed for new products, particularly in the vital field of consumer electronics.

The Reality of the 1990s

In the early 1990s, the much-vaunted Japanese "bubble-economy" burst. The highly inflated prices of Tokyo real-estate fell dramatically (although they remain exceptionally high by world standards), causing considerable difficulty for companies and financial institutions who counted land among their primary assets. A series of political and financial scandals caused great domestic turmoil and considerable international scrutiny, in part by Western observers who had repeatedly forecast an end to the Japanese post-war miracle and who saw in the financial mess of the 1990s confirmation of their pessimistic assumptions about the Japanese economy. Political turmoil, highlighted by the 1993 removal from office of the long-dominant Liberal Democratic Party, slowed the political and administrative response. And the often celebrated bureaucrats at the MITI and MOF were shown to be merely human in their ability to anticipate all the permutations of the fast-changing international economy.

While the state of the contemporary national economy will be dealt with in the next chapter, suffice it to say at this point that outside observers have historically been too quick to dismiss Japanese commercial and political resilience. Westerners underestimated Japan at the turn of the century and again in the 1930s. They assumed that it would take the country generations, not a decade, to rebound from the devastation of World War II. They anticipated that the oil crisis of the 1970s would undercut Japan's industrial base. And they forecast that the bubble economy of the 1980s would explode. That external observers have been consistently wrong about Japan's economic prospects does not, inevitably, mean they are wrong about their current pessimistic forecasts. It should, however, suggest caution in writing the Japanese off and in assuming that the spate of bad financial news (not that much more serious than the financial crisis that hit the United States in the 1980s following the collapse of the savings and loans sector) means that Japan's position as an economic superpower is under attack.

The Essence of Japanese Culture and Society

The very public transformation of Japan left outsiders with the superficial impression that all had changed. Where once the Emperor and shoguns had ruled, there were now democratic institutions. In a land once tied to the virtues of agriculture and rural life, cities virtually exploded into existence, and industrial labor (and industrial unrest) became an integral part of the social fabric. Western styles seemed to be replacing Japanese clothing, haircuts, and even food. But, and it is a very substantial but, not as

The Kin Kakuji Gold Temple is located in Kyoto.

much had changed as appeared on the surface. For underlying the transformation of Japanese society was a value system that continued to define the essence of Japan. These cultural norms were rooted in Japan's past and remained in place through the Meiji Revolution and beyond. More than changes in appearance and economic structures, the core values of Japanese society gave the country its character and determined the behavior of its people. It was here, not on the factory floor, or the halls of parliament, that one encountered the essence of Japan. While a full consideration of the central characteristics of Japanese society would take volumes to handle adequately, the following are some of the key elements:

1. **Japanese Homogeneity**   Japan is dominated by people of Japanese ancestry. While many other nations have culturally and ethnically mixed populations, over 99% of Japan's population is Japanese. (Of the non-Japanese 50% are Korean). Japan has made few efforts to incorporate newcomers into their society; even Koreans born and raised in Japan were, until very recently, denied full citizenship.

2. **Uchi and Soto (Inside and Outside)**   Underlying Japanese society are the concepts of uchi and soto. The goal in Japan is to be on the inside, to conform to the social expectations and codes of conduct. The inside group changes according to the circumstances; one can be inside a family, a company, or a nation. *Gaijin*, the long-standing word for foreigner, translates literally as "outside person." These concepts are important, for Japanese people act differently depending on whether they are dealing with someone in their group or outside their group.

3. **Japanese Distinctiveness**   The Japanese have placed such an emphasis on their uniqueness that many have come to believe that no one else can comprehend their culture, understand their values, or truly fit into their society. At its most extreme, this has emerged as a pseudo-science called *Nihonjin-ron*, or Japan theory, which attempts to provide plausible explanations for the distinctiveness of the Japanese and their fundamental differences from other groups of people.

4. **Japanese Education**   Japan's legendary and highly regimented education system is widely credited with being at the root of the country's economic miracle. The same competitive spirit that drives the national economy can be seen in the classroom, where students compete for spaces in prime kindergartens and keep competing until they secure a space in a prestigious

university. The Japanese education system is highly organized and ensures nationwide continuity and comparability. Students wear uniforms to school, teachers provide intense supervision of children, and parents pay for expensive after-school classes (*juku*, or cram schools) to ensure that their sons and daughters remain competitive. The school experience is capped off with the *shiken jigoku*, or examination hell, the competition for university entrance. Because of the importance attached to the prestige of specific universities, securing entry to a top-rank university generally means that the individual has gained access to an important government department or private sector company.

5. **The Japanese Language**   One of the reasons Japan seems to remain aloof from the rest of the world is the simple matter of language. While the Japanese borrowed much of their written language from Chinese, their language is not very close to any other modern tongue, thus separating them from their neighbors. The task of learning *kanji*, the characters that are the foundation of written communication, is time-consuming and onerous, and yet, Japan has one of the world's highest literacy rates and exceptionally high readerships for newspapers and books. The spoken language is similarly diverse, with a variety of speech levels that relate to the social status of the person being addressed. Westerners unfamiliar with kanji have long complained about the difficulty of adjusting to the written language and, in particular, to the challenges of navigating a city where all signs are in this complicated script. Take heart! Most popular transportation and shopping areas now have signs in kanji and *romaji* (an alphabetic transliteration of the Japanese text). Around Tokyo, signs in English are becoming increasingly common.

6. **Status and Social Rank** Drawing on centuries-old traditions of social order and status, Japanese society remains tightly structured around rank. Professional, age, or employment status generally determines social standing, and colleagues and subordinates are expected to comport themselves accordingly. A *sempai*, a veteran or senior member of a team or organization, is expected to look out for the *kohai*, or junior members. The latter, in turn, are expected to follow the sempai's lead and take instructions from him or her. Hierarchy and social order are highly esteemed within Japanese society, whether in the family or business setting. Deviations from accepted norms can cause extreme discomfort and unpleasantness. This is a standard problem for Western business people, whose casualness and lack of deference to elders can offend their Japanese counterparts.

7. **The Importance of the Group** Japanese society places a high premium on the group and, consequently, less importance on individuality and personal expression. Employees demonstrate remarkable loyalty to their companies, often working extremely long hours and then spending their Sunday break at a company event. The Japanese seek to protect harmony and to prevent conflict; considerable effort is devoted to developing a consensus on key decisions. This affinity for the group, which includes family, community, sports teams, company, city, or nation, fuels a great deal of activity and conditions their response to outside influences.

8. **Tatemae (Outward Appearance)** The Japanese seek to maintain external appearances and devote considerable effort to maintaining face. In their dealings with Westerners, Japanese business people are often described as being vague and indecisive; the "Yes that means No" is an all-too-familiar element

in commercial dealings. The Japanese do not like to make direct statements, particularly if they feel that their judgment will result in unhappiness or anger.

For years, outsiders have been seeking to understand the Japanese "mind" and have offered countless explanations for the country's uniqueness. Sometimes, they try too hard. Japanese social conventions are not precisely the same as those in other countries, even other Asian countries, but they are not particularly baffling. As a people, the Japanese are generally polite, easy to work with (particularly if you understand the imperatives that drive their actions, demeanor, and decision making processes), and make very reliable business partners.

Where Japan truly stands out is in the people's commitment to their nation and to economic success. Several times in the twentieth century, the Japanese have subordinated personal ambition to national accomplishment and have surrendered short-term, personal gains for long-term, national benefits. This ability and willingness to put the group first makes Japan significantly different from other industrialized nations. Business people from those countries where individualism dominates often have difficulty comprehending Japan and have trouble understanding a capitalist economic system that is not driven by a "me-first" philosophy. While this attitude, this celebration of the group over the individual, is deeply embedded in Japanese culture and history, it is one of the primary factors behind the country's continued economic achievements.

Japan is, in the final analysis, a truly special place. Visitors will see it in the wonderful blend of the modern and traditional, in the uniqueness of Japanese language and culture that stands alongside the ubiquitous contemporary technology, in the unpretentious mix of Western and Asian influences, and in the frantic pace of a nation committed to economic prosperity. This is a country, too, that has an extremely strong sense of history—

witness the annual migrations to key historic and cultural sites—and an equally strong eye on the future. The Japanese look well into the future when developing their corporate and national strategies, and are rarely bound up in the quarterly statement mentality that limits the flexibility and the vision of most Western firms.

CHAPTER 2

The Japanese Economy

Japan is the world's second largest economy after the United States, and few would have forecast this only fifty years ago. At the end of World War II, Japan was on its knees, crushed physically and psychologically. The cities, or what remained, stood in ruins. Most industries—and certainly all the key ones—had been bombed into oblivion, and the nation's age-old farms had been destroyed. Its citizens struggled to feed themselves; people literally starved to death in the aftermath of the conflict.

There was no clear path forward. Japan needed to trade in order to bring in the desperately needed foodstuffs. But the world was not in a forgiving mood in 1945 and held the land of the rising sun responsible for the international devastation of the war years. Japan had little to trade and, were it not for the benevolence of the United States, would have wallowed in despair and demoralization.

And then, fifty years later, the world looks on Japan's economy with envy. Japan is one of the most technologically advanced and innovative societies on earth. The country's products, once held in mild contempt, are now celebrated for their high quality, high standards, and good price. Two questions emerge: what happened over the last five decades that turned a vanquished nation into an economic colossus and how did this small, resource-poor country develop such a vibrant, creative and expansive economy?

Japan has few natural advantages, save for ready access to Asia and a strategic location in the North Pacific. The archipelago is small—roughly the size of California—but is home to about 126 million people, making it the eighth largest in the world. Although the country has a rich agrarian heritage, one that it clings to with nostalgic tenacity, it has little arable land. Since it opened

Matsumoto Castle is one of the best examples of Japan's rich cultural heritage.

its shores to foreign traders only 150 years ago, Japan has relied on the importation of vast quantities of the basic necessities, from food to oil. But the Japanese have one resource that few countries can match—a devoted, hard working labor force that is willing to surrender personal benefits for the prosperity of the nation. This national zeal has been combined with an influential and forward-looking civil service, which coordinates government activities, education, and corporate investment. The net effect, often critically called Japan Inc., is a country relentless in the pursuit of economic advantage and willing to make the personal and collective sacrifices necessary to succeed in a global economy.

At the end of the twentieth century, Japan stands as one of the world's greatest trading nations. Foreign companies are anxious to break into the rich and hitherto largely untapped domestic market, which is supported by one of the highest per capita incomes in the world. Japan's corporate hand can be seen around the globe, in South African forests, Canadian coal mines, New Zealand golf courses, German retail stores, and any of the thousands of other places where Japanese investments or Japanese products have found a niche. Japan's rise to prominence was not without its trials and difficult turns. Japan is now an economic power to be reckoned with, its major corporations are highly regarded international competitors, and the Japanese marketplace is an attractive lure for would-be exporters.

Challenges, Strengths, and Recent Changes
Opinions on the future of the Japanese economy are mixed. While there are commentators who suggest that the Japanese economy could surpass the American economy in the near future, there are others who loudly proclaim Japan's imminent demise as a trading nation and suggest that business people bypass Japan to do business with other countries in Asia. Let's examine the facts.

In 1996, Japan's gross national production represented 70% of the GNP of the rest of Asia combined, and fully 80% of the GNP of the United States, the world's most important economy and a nation more than twice as populous as Japan. Furthermore, Japanese per capita income is now approximately 36% higher than that of the United States. The vast majority of Japanese citizens (90% by a recent poll) consider themselves to be middle class; only slightly more than 5% feel that they are members of the lower class. Fortune Magazine's Global 500, which listed the top corporations for 1996, included 140 Japanese firms. Japanese savings, the cornerstone of the national economy, accounts for over 40% of the world's total savings.

Challenges
So, what are some of the problems to which the pessimists point?

Aging Population Japan has the most rapidly aging population on earth. Experts estimate that by early in the next century almost one-quarter of the Japanese population will be over the age of 64. (In comparison, the United States, which is also concerned about its aging population, is looking at 18% of its citizens being over 64 at this time.) Japan's aging population, combined with a low birth rate and little migration, pose the threat of a significant decline in the country's overall population. Some writers have suggested that the Japanese population could decline dramatically (some claim to as low as 50 million people) by the year 2050.

The implications of this aging population are enormous. Demand for health care and additional services for the elderly are already skyrocketing. Japan's traditionally tight government pension schemes are under attack by increasingly influential numbers of seniors. Just when the country can least afford to increase pensions, political necessity may leave the government no option. With 25% of the population retired, it will be up to those workers who are left to pay the taxes to support the increased need for social services. Companies could also be short of labor as significant numbers of their workers retire. This may not be as large a problem as it initially appears, however, as Japan has been investing heavily in robots and automation. Japan may well replace many of its existing workers with automated forms of production.

Disarray in the Financial System The 1990s has seen a variety of scandals and bankruptcies in Japan's financial systems. These began with the fallout from the heady years of the late 1980s, which had seen the vast expansion of domestic demand—a growth in capital investments and in personal spending. (The boom, often referred to as the "bubble economy" lasted for four-and-a-half years until the middle of 1990 when its foundation of unrealistically high real estate values collapsed.) The bursting of the bubble led to untold numbers of bankruptcies and a banking sector that was drastically overextended.

In late 1997, bankruptcies again rocked the financial world. A number of blue-chip financial institutions declared bankruptcy. These included Sanyo Securities Corporation, Hokkaido Takushoku Bank and, most startlingly, Yamaichi Securities, one of Japan's big four brokerage houses. Embarrassing scandals—and in Japan, the ignominy comes as much from being caught as it does from the act of corruption itself—have continued. Corporate malfeasance includes a number of instances of paying gangsters not to disturb annual general meetings and compensating special corporate clients for trading losses.

Housing In Japan's large cities, the shortage of affordable housing is a serious concern. Space is at a premium, and many people live in very small, cramped quarters. It has been said that some young women have decided against having children because of their inability to offer them a decent life in such a crowded urban setting.

Sociologists now argue that Japanese society is increasingly being divided into those who own property and those who do not. One-hundred-year mortgages are now being signed, ensuring that the next generation inherits a substantial mortgage as well as a house.

Japan's Relations with the United States   Japan's substantial trade surplus with the United States has been a bone of contention with the Americans for years. The United States has been pressuring the Japanese government to liberalize and deregulate its markets. Tensions over trade issues have come close to precipitating a serious breach on numerous occasions. While the Japanese have begun deregulating, what has been done to date is nowhere near adequate for the Americans and Japanese, and Western perceptions of what constitutes deregulation often differ. (Glen Fukushima, Vice President of the American Chamber of Commerce in Japan and Vice President of AT&T, notes that deregulation is often mistranslated into Japanese to mean "an easing or relaxation of regulations" rather than a complete elimination of rules.)

Japan's focus is always on what is in the country's best interest. There is little question that in certain strategic industries at least, the Japanese government protects its own industries. How the United States reacts to Japan in the years ahead will be of fundamental importance. It is, after all, Japan's largest export market by a substantial margin and Japan's largest source of imports. If the United States were to become more protective, to make it a little more difficult for Japanese companies to sell there unless certain concessions were made in return, Japan's economic life could well become more difficult.

The United States is also upset with Japan's failure to assume a significant military and diplomatic role on the international scene. Since the end of World War II, Japan has played a rather quiet back seat role internationally. Article 9 of the Japanese Constitution renounces war and limits Japan's military to that of a Self Defense Force (although this SDF is the sixth largest armed force in the

Commuter railways and subways remain vital to the Japanese economy and figure prominently in the urban landscapes of the country.

world). Japan's decision to donate money but not send troops to the Gulf War of 1991 unleashed international criticism. As did the fact that, until very recently, Japan did not even participate in peace keeping missions. Now that Japan is an economic powerhouse, other nations believe it is time for the country to play a stronger role, both militarily and generally, in world affairs.

Strengths

Although the country faces formidable challenges, Japan is able to count on an impressive array of national attributes. These characteristics helped Japan rebound from the failures of World War II and establish itself as a major international power.

Manufacturing Base Japan's exports are overwhelmingly dominated by manufactured products. The country's major exports are high value-added manufactured products, particularly machinery, electrical machines, and vehicles. Those three categories, which make up 65% of all of Japan's exports, include goods ranging from industrial robots to facsimile machines, and from computer parts to television equipment. Other major exports include optical and medical instruments, ships and boats, as well as iron and steel (including iron and steel products.)

High Technology   Even more important than Japan's emphasis on manufacturing is the kind of manufacturing it emphasizes. Japan has been moving more and more toward the production of the most highly sophisticated manufactured products. The high values of the yen since the late 1980s means that the labor intensive production of various low and middle range value-added products is no longer cost effective. Japanese corporations began moving their factories overseas, initially to North America to circumvent protectionist feelings and tariffs, and most recently to Asia. The industries that have remained in Japan have been those on the

Japan's road network, particularly in Tokyo, has not kept pace with the increase in traffic, making it difficult to move quickly around the major cities.

high value-added end. Japanese manufacturing prowess and emphasis on market share at all costs has put the country in charge of a wide range of industries and technologies. Eammon Fingleton, a Tokyo-based journalist and author of *Blindside. Why Japan is On Track to Overtake the United States by the Year* 2000, discusses in detail the sectors that Japan dominates directly (robotics, cameras, auto industry manufacturing equipment, copiers, musical instruments, superconductivity, energy efficient transportation technologies, and others) or through its domination of key components (notebook computers, printers, compact disk players, semi-conductor materials and equipment, supercomputers, cellular phones, fax machines, optical scanning equipment, and others.) It is these manufacturing strengths, and in many cases monopolies, which underpin the Japanese economy and give it the financial resources to deal with difficulties it may have to face.

The Japanese Bureaucracy While a few people argue that Japan achieved its enormous economic success *despite* the famous Japanese bureaucracy, most are quite willing to give at least some credit to the well-known MITI and the lesser known but more powerful MOF. The bureaucrats in these ministries have long been in charge of guiding Japan's economy. Usually referred to as industrial policy, the Japanese government, and these ministries in particular, have frequently intervened in the market to promote rapid industrial growth, most often through an emphasis on manufacturing. From the 1950s through the 1970s, the government protected new industries with import restrictions and direct subsidies until Japanese manufacturers were strong enough to compete with foreign competitors. (For example, import restrictions on trucks and buses were lifted in 1961, those on cars in 1965, and those on color film in 1971.) The government helped industries in temporary difficulties to restructure and those with more permanent problems to diversify into other sectors. Preferential access to foreign exchange, raw materials, and financial assistance were other tools MITI used to help key industries.

As part of the conditions for entry into the General Agreement on Tariffs and Trade (GATT), Japan had to indicate that it was liberalizing its imports and eliminating tariffs and import quotas. Government strategy, therefore, had to shift to less direct means of support and leadership—administrative guidance. MITI used this administrative guidance to convince companies to do what the ministry thought was in the best interests of Japan. This ranged from encouraging the formation of mergers to suggesting companies move out of declining industries to organizing industry-wide research projects. While MITI did not get everything right (the most widely cited "mistake" was MITI's attempt in the 1950s to limit the Japanese automobile industry to only one or two companies), most of the industries the ministry targeted were successful and subsequently formed the backbone of Japan's economic growth.

MOF activities are more focused on the big picture. Through various regulations, it has ensured that Japan's saving rate is high and that this money is available for industrial investment. Domestic consumption is suppressed by making it difficult to obtain certain services or products. (A good example of this would be the extraordinarily high cost of air travel originating in Japan—a direct reflection of government policy and not simply market forces. Despite the fact that trips from Japan cost much more than the same flight originating elsewhere, during peak times all flights are completely sold out. If extra runways were built and more flights made available, more Japanese would travel.) The bonus system of payment, whereby employees receive a relatively small monthly salary but twice a year receive lump sum payments equal to three or four months salary, encourages people to live on their monthly salary and save their bonus payments for large purchases.

The Japanese Population   Japan has a well-disciplined, hard working labor force. People are expected to put their employers before their personal lives and are required to display intense loyalty to the company. (While some commentators note that young people today value family life more and will not be willing to put their companies first, the same thing has been written numerous time over the last few decades. Attitudes may be shifting slightly, but generally, the company for whom one works is still of extreme importance and, for most male employees, the main priority.) Japanese employees willingly work long hours (often on top of lengthy and tiring daily commutes) and take few holidays. The average Japanese worker only takes about half of his or her allotted vacation time.

Through the education system with its emphasis on rote learning and memorization, and in the early years with a company, the Japanese employee learns patience. A commitment to service, an ability to take orders, and a tenacious eye for detail all characterize the average Japanese employee.

While most long-term full time company employees are male, the main Japanese consumer is female. Japanese women look after the money in a marriage, and they make most of the purchasing decisions. Like their husbands, they are also detail oriented and quality conscious.

Perhaps the quality of vital importance in the Japanese population (which has already been pointed out but no harm in reiterating this point) is the people's ability (not always without a certain amount of government prompting) to sacrifice short-term personal pleasure for long-term national gains. As one journalist commented:

> "Many of the world's problems boil down to requiring today's generation to make sacrifices to ensure a more secure future for future generations. That is a tough choice for a Western

democracy, but one that Confucianism instinctively approaches with the right mindset."

— Eamon Fingleton, Blindside, p 352

Recent Changes in the Japanese Economy

Focus On Domestic Demand   In the last decade, the Japanese market and the Japanese consumer have assumed increasing importance. Japanese companies are making more of their products with their domestic market in mind. In fact, many products sold in Japan never even make it overseas. Kenneth Courtis, strategist and senior economist for the Deutsche Bank Group in Asia, points out that

> "From 1975 to 1985, the period of Japan's export boom, about three-quarters of innovation-related investment was targeted at the development of new products and services designed to penetrate the North American and European markets. Since 1986, however, there has been a complete reversal, with about 80 percent of innovation investment now targeting the domestic market. This means that new products and services will increasingly be introduced in Japan first. In short, Japan is positioning itself to play a role in the world economy similar to that which the United States played in the 1950s and 1960s. Then, new products were first developed and introduced into the American market, and as the international product life cycle unfolded, were released in sequence around the world. Over the 1990s, Japan will move to occupy a similar role as the new product laboratory for the world economy."
>
> — Doing Business in Japan, p 8

Some of the more innovative consumer items doing well in Japan include the head cooling pillow for hot summer nights, refrigerators with five or six compartments, each with a different cooling system for a different type of food, sensor-controlled mirrors to bring natural sunlight into dark buildings, low tables with a heat source below and a quilt over top to trap warm air for homes without central heating, and answering machines to discourage obscene phone calls (push a button and a threatening male voice yells out or a 100 decibel blast shrieks into the caller's ear). Other larger and more commercial products include temporary sidewalks (standard modular concrete curb pieces that are inexpensive and easy to install and, therefore, useful during road construction projects), a car wash that takes up only 360 square feet, automated downtown parking towers (a Ferris-wheel style elevator rotates cars and empty spaces up and down the parking tower), and capsule office buildings and hotels (with individual working or sleeping compartments.)

Several decades ago, the Japanese used to take the lead in consumer goods from Western, primarily North American producers. Now, the wealthy, highly selective Japanese consumer is looking for goods designed specifically for Japanese tastes and interests. Unique food and restaurant ideas are mushrooming in the country. Consumers can buy apples inscribed with personal messages that have been grown into the fruit, ice cream with flavors such as sweet potato, basil leaf, blue cheese, and oolong tea, as well as curry donuts and hot cocoa with chili sauce. Theme restaurants (multi-course meals all focused on one ingredient such as garlic or bamboo shoots); bars where you pay for the time spent, not the alcohol consumed; rental restaurants where customers come in and cook their own food for large parties (an opportunity for company executives to show off their culinary skills); bars with nurseries; cook-it-yourself restaurants; and restaurants where noodles float down chutes in front of customers who grab them with their chopsticks are some examples of the growing variety of Japanese dining experiences. The Japanese consumer is discerning and expects the products to meet local tastes, customs, and desires.

The Changing Nature of Japanese Trade   Until the mid-1980s, Japan was primarily an importer of raw materials and barely processed goods. In fact, over two-thirds of Japan's imports in 1985 were resource products. The rapid escalation in the value of the yen caused this to change as some of Japan's factories shifted offshore and as Japanese consumers became more interested in foreign products. By 1991, only 51% of Japan's imports were resource products, leaving 49% in the manufacturing sectors. By 1995, manufactured imports had increased an additional 10%, climbing to over 59% of total imports. The import categories with the largest increases were clothing, vehicles, electrical machinery, and miscellaneous manufactures, including toys, jewelry, and art. This shift in trading patterns creates enormous opportunities for foreign manufacturers and processors, provided that the products take into account the Japanese demand for high quality and adjustments for national consumer tastes.

Deregulation Under pressure from the Keidanren (the Federation of Economic Organizations in Japan) and the business community, the Japanese government began deregulating the Japanese economy in 1993. (The first action program was actually announced by Prime Minister Nakasone in July 1985 but little progress was made.) In March 1995, the government announced its "Deregulation Action Plan," which outlined its strategy for reviewing a variety of regulations. Government rules under review include regulations on housing construction materials, telecommunications, and packaging and distribution of food products. The government has put measures in place to reform its procurement system and to encourage foreign firms to enter the Japanese market. After the October 1996 elections, Prime Minister Hashimoto announced even more reforms, designed to change the laws relating to banking, securities, insurance, and foreign exchange and make Tokyo an international market. The crises in Japanese financial institutions in the years 1997–1998, caused in part by Japanese exposure in Asian markets, drew attention to the slow pace of government reforms in the financial sector and gave impetus to the changes.

Practical Implications
So, what are some of the practical implications for business people of this overview of the Japanese economy?

Selected Countries Ranked According to Per Capita Gross National Product, Purchasing Power Parity, 1997 est.

	(Unit: USD)
Luxembourg	33,700
United States	30,200
Norway	27,400
Singapore	24,600
Japan	**24,500**
Switzerland	23,800
Denmark	23,200
France	22,700
Austria	21,400
Germany	20,800

Source: CIA World Fact Book, 1998.

1. It is vital to note that the Japanese economy is still strong— despite dire forecasts of the country's fiscal and economic crises. While talk of Japan's financial woes and economic recession dominate Western discussions of Japan, a closer look reveals that the second largest economy is, and promises to remain, a powerful economic force. Japan now represents 20% of the world's GNP. Its 126 million quality conscious consumers have a per capita income 36% higher than their American counterparts. (Note that the table adjusts income statistics for purchasing power parity and does not indicate absolute per capita income values.) During the first seven years of the 1990s, the period of Japan's so-called "recession", current account

surpluses totaled $655 billion, a dramatic increase from the $192 billion for the same period in the 1980s.

2. The Japanese continue to believe that their economic future lies in manufacturing. The appreciation of the yen, however, has meant that production of labor intensive low and middle value added products can no longer be produced in Japan cost effectively. Japanese companies have, therefore, shifted many of their factories offshore. Products that continue to be produced in Japan are those that are the most technologically sophisticated and the highest value added. These high technology products are also the strategic sectors upon which the Japanese government wishes the country to place its emphasis. As many foreign companies have discovered, competing with the Japanese in strategic products or services is difficult. (That there is a difference on access to the Japanese market for foreign firms depending on whether or not they fall within the strategic category is well illustrated by an American Chamber of Commerce forum in Japan. Here nine American company representatives described their companys' experiences in Japan. Those selling consumer products or providing non-strategic services reported no difficulties while those with products considered strategic expressed various degrees of dissatisfaction with trade barriers.)

For companies competing in the high technology sectors that overlap with Japan, the road to success in the Japanese market will be long and arduous. However, for those corporations in low end manufacturing or service industries, opportunities continue to increase dramatically. High labor costs and international frustration with Japan's trade surplus forced the country to recognize that it cannot produce everything. Japan's goal, then, is to produce those items at the top of the value-added pyramid. This leaves the door open for foreign companies to sell many of the other products Japan no longer considers strategic.

3. While this book only touches on the role of the Japanese government, it would be worthwhile to make sure your company understands how the bureaucracy operates. The most crucial point to note is that the Japanese bureaucracy is committed to looking after Japan's best interests. To determine, therefore, what a company will be able to successfully sell in Japan, it is worthwhile, maybe even vital, to understand how to make products or plans that will be attractive to the Japanese bureaucracy. Making sure the product contains Japanese parts that will therefore be sold worldwide might be one method of achieving this goal.

4. Additional opportunities are emerging in the Japanese market. Japan's rapidly aging population, for example, has spawned a need for products and services for the elderly. These could range from health care products and barrier-free buildings to international travel for seniors. The deregulation of the financial sector could open up possibilities for firms in this area. New markets are developing in such sectors as processed foods, organic fruits and vegetables, consumer products, speciality restaurants, and computer software.

5. To actually set up operations in Japan, the hiring of employees might be one of the first challenges to overcome. Interviews with Westerners in foreign companies in Japan reveal that finding good quality Japanese employees is indeed a big problem. As will be discussed later, a Japanese company generally offers an employee more prestige and security than a foreign one. As Japanese tend to stay with one company for a

long time, taking a job with a non-Japanese company is a risk. In addition, the skills and qualities that the foreign company is looking out for (for example, the ability to work on one's own without direction) might not be the kind of skills most Japanese are best trained. Foreign companies might be well advised to look into the possibility of hiring women. Most women in the Japanese workforce are under utilized. There are many bright, well-educated women who could be quite easily enticed to work for a foreign company.

6. For reasons that will become clear as we proceed, it is vital to recognize that the root elements in Japanese culture permeate the business community and will have a profound impact on your attempts to trade in Japan. For example, a commitment to detail and to planning can make Japanese business people seem formidable. The Japanese like to understand every angle of a situation, and questions will be asked about even the tiniest of details. This penchant for detail, for forward-planning, and for constant checking is deeply embedded in Japanese culture. For your part, recognize that your Japanese counterparts will be well prepared. An attempt to match the same level of detailed knowledge of their business would be a good start.

In the next chapter, we will look more closely at life inside a Japanese corporation. A general understanding of the background of the Japanese with whom you may be doing business either as a joint venture partner, a competitor, a supplier, or as a consumer can help you become more effective in your business dealings.

CHAPTER 3

Inside a Japanese Company

An understanding of Japan's corporate culture is important to those who want to do business with the Japanese. While a short overview cannot do justice to the complexity of Japanese business structures, values, and attitudes, it can point out some of the fundamental differences between Japanese and Western practices and help anticipate some of the misunderstandings that could otherwise occur. As with most books discussing Japanese management techniques, this survey will focus on the characteristics of larger Japanese corporations. Although only about one-third of the Japanese work for such companies, the management structure of the larger companies sets the tone for the country and the workforce and is therefore worthy of a close scrutiny.

Many of the small- and medium-sized companies, however, cannot afford the benefits and structures that the large companies employ. During economic downturns, these smaller companies experience more of the layoffs and shutdowns than do the larger corporations. In addition, the tough economic times of the late 1990s have seen some changes to life even in the large corporations. As it is too early to gauge the extent or permanence of these changes, bear in mind that what follows describes the way traditional Japanese companies have operated in the post-World War II period. At the end of the chapter is a brief description and some examples of ways companies are responding to the new economic realities.

For a start, shareholders have little control or ownership of Japanese companies. Company debt to equity ratios can be as high as 80:20. Ownership rests with financial institutions, while daily control is in the hands of corporate executives. Financial institutions are backed by the Bank of Japan behind which stands the government and a huge pool of national savings. (As will be discussed toward the end of the chapter, banking failures of the late 1990s have severely strained this arrangement.) The Japanese rate of personal savings is very high. Statistics for 1996 revealed that Japanese saved 12.8% of their earnings, while the Germans saved 11.6%, French 9.2%, Canadians 7.9%, the British 5.7%, and Americans 4.7%. Japan's high savings rate can be partly attributed to its wage bonus system through which employees receive a twice-a-year bonus (in December and June) of about two to four months' salary. As people are used to living on their monthly salaries, these bonuses are frequently saved and put toward major purchases. More important than the bonus system argues at least one commentator on Japan is governmental efforts at suppressing consumption (by, for example, limiting imports, denying air links to popular foreign destinations, and restricting consumer credit) and forcing people to save.

Keiretsu

Many large Japanese companies are tied together as members of various *keiretsu*, or business groupings that consist of numerous companies. Companies in a variety of sectors, their subsidiaries, suppliers, distributors, and subcontractors make up a keiretsu. At the core is usually a bank, and most of these business groupings contain firms in over 20 industries in fields as diverse as chemicals, real estate, electronics, and insurance. Each keiretsu tries to represent as complete a cross-section of the Japanese economy as possible. The goal is to have one, and only one company, in each type of business. As Hitotsubashi University's Takatoshi Ito once described:

"A modern enterprise (*keiretsu*) group is a collection of firms which hold shares in one another, borrow from the financial institution in the group and behave strategically as a group." (p 180)

Interlocking shares and directorates tie together the various companies. This reciprocal shareholding keeps ownership within the group for political, not commercial reasons; to ensure that shares are held and not sold. This affords the keiretsu companies security from hostile takeovers, giving them the freedom to make long-term plans. Companies in the Mitsubishi keiretsu have the highest ratio of interlocking shares—about 27% of the average Mitsubishi firm is owned by other Mitsubishi firms.

Keiretsu firms behave like members of a club. They work hard to keep business within the group, and they look out for each other. There are six large keiretsu today: Mitsui, Mitsubishi, Sumitomo, Fuyo, Sanwa, and Ikkan. The first three have their roots in the pre-war zaibatsu, which the occupation blamed for contributing to the Japanese war effort and disbanded. The member companies in these three keiretsu have particularly strong and close relationships. The Fuyo, Sanwa, and Ikkan groups were formed after the war and have powerful banks at their centre. The exact organizational structure and the control exerted on member companies vary from group to group, but the obligation to extend mutual aid and to keep as much business as possible within the keiretsu family is consistently strong. There are also other types of business groups, which usually include a manufacturing firm and its myriad of suppliers and distributors. These kinds of groups are more vertically integrated and, therefore, do not have a member bank. Sony would be the best example of this type of business group. It has 87 subsidiaries and affiliated companies and owns shares in most of them.

The keiretsu structure is an example of the role and importance of the group in Japanese business culture. The Japanese enjoy the feeling of belonging to a group and working together for a common purpose. For the most part, the miracle of the post-war Japanese economy has been attributed to the commitment demonstrated by the entire Japanese population to the success of their companies and to rebuilding Japan. This devotion to nation and company influences employee-employer attitudes and relations. It has meant a stronger bond between the company and the worker.

Companies feel a strong sense of responsibility to their employees and make a long-term commitment to them. Stories abound of senior managers voluntarily taking pay cuts before contemplating laying off any line workers. Most Japanese who work for major Japanese corporations expect to have a job for most of their working lives. Although the often used term "lifetime employment" exaggerates the reality (many firms have been retiring more and more young workers, particularly recently, often leaving them without enough money on which to comfortably retire), this job security has made most employees loyal and hard working. Even employees who work for smaller Japanese companies have a tendency to stay with the same company for long periods; the average number of years spent with a company in 1996 was 12.7 years for men and 7.4 for women.

Part of the Family

To build and enforce this loyalty, companies try to create a family atmosphere for their employees. They work hard to make employees feel part of this corporate "family." Japanese managers take a great interest in their employees' lives, offering advice and guidance with personal problems, acting as a matchmaker for unmarried employees, and attending weddings and graduations. If an employee gets into legal trouble, his or her manager will apologize to the injured party and the authorities on behalf of the company.

Accommodations in company dormitories for single employees and families, subsidized housing in company subdivisions or apartment buildings are available. Some female-only dormitories, especially those in rural areas, still have curfews (as early as 10 p.m.!) and rules that most Westerners might find stifling. (These originate from the time when a company gave its commitment to parents to be responsible for the young girls it hires.)

Companies sponsor a variety of sporting and recreational activities and teams. Classes in English, tea ceremony, and *ikebana*, or flower arranging, are held in the evenings. Male co-workers often go out drinking and socializing together, and there are company picnics and outings to corporate lodges at ski resorts or near famous *onsen*, or Japanese hot springs.

Novel Ways of Maintaining Family Ties

The Japanese family has been under considerable pressure in recent years. The combination of smaller houses (which make it harder for extended families to live together) and intense work pressure has created serious gaps between generations. Japanese companies, however, have been creative in their efforts to remedy the situation. One Japanese firm provides a unique service: they pay professional actors to play the role of son/daughter, spouse, or children for aging grandparents who have limited contact with their own families. Another company takes a portrait of a child and a tape recording of his/her voice and produces a look- and sound-alike doll, complete with a microchip recorder, to compensate grandparents who do not get to see enough of their grandchildren.

Work days often begin with group calisthenics and the recitation of the company motto or the yelling of the corporate cheer. In return for long-time employment and this familial security, companies expect hard work, loyalty, and unswerving commitment from their employees. Few workers find this loyalty difficult to reciprocate, as a job with a large important company is very prestigious and highly sought after. For some employees, the company will hold overwhelming significance throughout their lives, even replacing their personal lives. A documentary on *karoshi*, or death from overwork, illustrated this dramatically. It showed an interview with a Japanese wife discussing her husband's collapse and subsequent stroke. After the stroke, she said he could not remember her name or the names of any of their children. In fact, the only word he could remember was the name of the company for which he had worked!

Hiring and Firing Staff

Recruitment of staff for Japanese companies is handled quite consistently. Companies hire once a year and almost exclusively at the entry level. New employees join companies annually on April 1st upon completion of either high school (for blue collar workers) or university (for white collar workers). All new employees are, therefore, about the same age with similar experiences of life. Almost none will have traveled, worked, gone to graduate school, or had any experiences to differentiate themselves from their fellow recruits. Japanese companies prefer to hire generalists rather than specialists and to train their employees in-house. Graduate school tends to be only for those students seeking an academic career, although companies will send promising employees who have been with the company for a number of years overseas (usually to the United States) to earn a master of business administration degree. The goal of in-house training is to immerse their new staff in the company philosophy and way of thinking while teaching them the technical and professional skills they need.

This in-house training begins as soon as the new recruits start work. Often, the first few months up to the first year of employment are spent in a training program. The structure of this initial training varies among companies, but the objective—to develop company loyalty—is the same. Some companies send their new employees to a kind of army boot camp; others send them on a lengthy retreat with corporate pep talks, meditation sessions, and intensive exercise regimes. For the male white collar employees of Toyota Motor Corporation, initial training takes seven months. Based out of Toyota's Toyota City headquarters in Aichi prefecture, recruits spend two weeks learning the basic structure of a car and the company's philosophy. For the next three weeks, they work on the factory floor as an assembly line worker. Toyota uses this training to stress that the most important part about the company is its products and the efficient way they are produced. The company hopes that by ensuring that every single male employee has worked "on the line," all future company business managers and engineers will not forget what life is like for a factory worker. After completing the factory training, the next three months are spent in sales, where employees learn the retail end of the car business. Most of these sales are actually still conducted by going door-to-door.

This initial training period forms the foundation of an employee's experience with his or, in some instances, her company. (For most women who occupy support role positions and resign upon marriage, training is limited to a few weeks and focuses on polite language and manners.) As companies hire primarily at the entry level, it is difficult for people to jump from one big Japanese company to another. As loyalty is the most highly valued quality, someone who is considering switching jobs is automatically suspect. Some job hopping does occur, usually early on in a career or to a foreign company, but leaving a company position is not easy:

> "For a Japanese supervisor, losing a valued employee is a black mark. Major Japanese companies which consider employee solidarity one of their greatest strengths, put intense pressure on workers to remain loyal. Supervisors rarely can offer their people big raises in return for staying, since that would disrupt tightly controlled pay scales. So they yell at departing subordinates. They lock them in rooms and badger them. Sometimes they even appeal directly to the employees' families. Among conservative Japanese, a job-hopper may be viewed as a bit of a traitor and more than one would-be defector has stayed put because of intense family and peer pressure."

— *Wall Street Journal*, September 9, 1986

Employee Advancement

New employees in each year's cohort progress through their careers in rank and salary in tandem with each other. Advancement up the corporate ladder occurs primarily as a function of age-seniority for at least the first 10 years a worker is with a company. Individual differences in wages and promotions do not become evident until after the first decade of employment (when the first of the cohort are promoted to section heads), and even then, the salary differences are minimal and can depend on other variables such as family situation. This makes it difficult for employees to compare themselves with others and is designed to keep candidates thinking they are in the promotion race, and therefore working harder, for a longer period.

Even the weakest employee will eventually reach the *kakaricho*, or section head, level, and most will become a *kacho*, or manager, which is the next rung up the ladder. Further up, nearer the top of the hierarchy, some employees are selected for the general manager, director, and chief executive positions in succession, while others receive positions in related companies or retire. As a general rule, no one reports to a person of the same age group or younger so that once people of one entry year start being promoted to the more senior positions, others from that year will be retiring. The belief is that bosses will be better able to support younger employees if they know their subordinates will never be usurping their positions.

Within this system of long-term employment, there are naturally those who, by virtue of laziness or incompetence, do not pull their weight. Often called *madogiwazoku* (the window seat tribe, referring to the fact that these people are often relegated to seats by the window), they keep their jobs and their desks but are given little work or responsibility. (This is an interesting difference from the Western perspective that an office or a desk with a view out the window is a symbol of status!) From the company's point of view, the costs involved in keeping an inactive and inefficient employee on staff are overshadowed by the broader, collective benefits of demonstrating company loyalty to its employees, as well as its commitment to job security.

Labor Unions

Labor unions operate quite differently in Japan. Most large Japanese companies have enterprise unions that represent the employees in one company rather than those in an entire industry. Therefore if one union strikes, the production for its company stops, but production by competitors in the same industry does not. This, naturally, would enable these other companies to grab the customers of the company on strike. As there is little the union could gain by this, strikes of any length of time are exceedingly rare. Unions must work with management to achieve the long-term goals of the company. Strikes are used primarily to indicate to management that the union is upset. Usually, the company and the public are notified of the strike ahead of time, and often, they are as short as one day or even fifteen minutes!

Each year in March, employers' associations and union federations meet together to negotiate base-rate salary increases (as a percentage) for all employees, which each company then strives to reach. This event is called *Shunto*, or Spring Labor Offensive, and tries to minimize the conflict involved in reaching wage settlements. Enterprise Unions and Shunto developed in response to a number of violent and debilitating industry-wide strikes of the 1960s. While much more peaceful company-worker relationships have resulted, there are complaints that the close-union management relations have left few options for workers with legitimate grievances.

Mandatory retirement in Japan was 55 for a long time but increased to 57 and in the last decade to 60. The government may even extend it to 65. Many companies, however, have begun retiring workers who are much younger. For many of these workers, though, financial concerns mean that retirement does not signal the end of work. Companies are not required to set up pension plans, so most employees receive a lump sum separation payment. Depending on the size and wealth of the company and the number of years of service, this separation payment can range from an amount adequate to start a small business to one too small to live on even for a short period of time. Sometimes, companies keep these "retired" workers as temporary employees at reduced wages and benefits.

Job Rotation

Job rotation is another important aspect of life in a Japanese corporation. Employees do not remain in one division for their careers; instead, they move from one division to another, approximately every five years. Experiences in many different parts of the company are gained this way so that by the time people reach senior management positions, they have an excellent macro sense of the company. While critics argue that this system means that no one has a particular area of expertise, others argue that this is more than offset by senior management's increased understanding of the goals and needs of the broad organization. For a foreign business person, what is most crucial to recognize is that the most senior Japanese person handling certain negotiations, for example, may not be the person most familiar with the technical details of the specific project. Although senior, he (not usually she) may have just transferred in from another division and be relying on his junior staff to recommend the best course of action. This means that presentations and explanations should be directed at the whole Japanese group.

No Detail is Too Small

Specific job descriptions are rare in Japanese companies. Rather than contracts or job descriptions outlining a person's individual duties, employees are simply expected to do what needs to be done. To a much greater extent than their Western counterparts, employees feel and can be held responsible for the activities of their departments and even their companies. Giving excuses or complicated explanations for tardiness or incomplete work is simply not done. Japanese employees simply apologize. No excuse will really be good enough, so there is no point in making one. This sense of responsibility and desire not to make mistakes cause Japanese employees to be fanatical about the tiniest of details and to continuously check to ensure that nothing goes wrong. *Kakunin denwa*, or confirmation phone calls, are common as employees want to make sure that whatever meeting has been arranged will occur as scheduled. Mark Zimmerman in his book, *How to Do Business with the Japanese*, also attributes some of this focus on detail to the Japanese education system:

> "But one major consequence of the system that a business person must be aware of is that the study habits a Japanese salary man began acquiring when he was five make him a compulsive doer of homework. No detail is too small for him to go over; no bit of information is considered irrelevant when studying a problem. He regards absolutely nothing as too much trouble. This capacity for study means that if you are dealing with a Japanese businessman, you can be sure that his preparation for the meeting will always be five steps ahead of yours. They have no concept of the favorite American pastime of 'winging it.' From preparing for business meetings to preparing to enter a foreign market, the Japanese executive's capacity for sheer doggedness is immense. This is perhaps one of the main reasons why the Japanese know so much more about us and our markets than we do about them." (p 19)

Before a new project is undertaken, the Japanese spend a great deal of time planning and consulting extensively with all the parties involved. The goal is to ensure that the project is well thought out and that it meshes with other company activities and goals. By consulting with all the interested groups, it is hoped that conflict will be minimized and a consensus to proceed achieved. The

Japanese refer to this behind-the-scenes consultation as *nemawashi*, which literally means "to cut around a tree before transplanting it" as opposed to roughly pulling out the tree by its roots, the equivalent of senior management simply imposing a decision. The Japanese hope that by the time a meeting is scheduled to take place, everyone involved has been consulted and whether or not there is support for the project has been determined. Therefore, once a decision to proceed has been reached, the Japanese move quickly.

Western companies often operate very differently and can therefore become quite frustrated with their Japanese counterparts. It can appear to take the Japanese an extremely long time to reach a basic decision, while the non-Japanese company often makes a quick initial decision, planning to research the details and consult with others as the project progresses. When the Japanese finally come back with the decision to proceed, they are ready to move quickly and become annoyed with the slow and casual responses to their detailed queries.

The emphasis that Japanese management places on planning and on the long term means that in Japanese offices there is often less concern over the short term waste of time, energy, and even talent. New employees are often expected to spend some of their time simply absorbing the company philosophy and learning through observation. While Western companies tend to see idle employees as an unnecessary expense, Japanese companies know they will make good use of these employees over the long haul. They are therefore not particularly concerned about their idleness in the early period of their employment. As patience is a virtue well utilized during the Japanese employees' career, it is worthwhile learning early. The continual planning, rewriting, and revising that is required will reinforce this patience over the years. It also encourages employees to participate in the day-to-day workings of an organization. It can, however, dampen youthful enthusiasm and stifle the desire to create, invent, and innovate.

Offices—An Open Plan

Offices have an open concept to facilitate the consultative process of the Japanese. While a couple of the most senior people have individual offices, the rest of the employees have desks in the middle of one large room. Desks are set up in long rows facing each other, and at the end, facing the rows perpendicularly, is the manager's desk for that particular section. One or two rows of desks make up the staff of one *ka*, or section, and three or four sections make up one *bu*, or department. On one floor of an office building, there could be two or three departments. Each department would contain about 50 people. A fair number of these employees, perhaps 15 or 20, would be OLs, or Office Ladies. Mostly women, they are responsible for photocopying documents, making and serving tea, performing simple tasks on the computer, and providing assistance in general office operations. Employees are seated by seniority, based on the number of years with the company. The older and more senior employees sit further up the row of desks closer to the manager. Just by a glance at the seating arrangements, a visitor would be able to determine, at least generally, who joined the company when.

These seating arrangements, while clearly not quiet and contemplative, are conducive to Japanese decision making, which involves lots of discussion and interaction. Although not always considered the most efficient model of office management, Japanese decision making is based on the continual generation of ideas by junior employees and a complicated formal authorization process. New ideas are subject to lengthy discussions among co-workers and supervisors and then developed into proposals. These proposals are circulated for approval up the row of desks to the section head and then to the manager. If any changes are requested, the proposal goes back down to the employee, changes are made, and goes through the process again until approved by the manager. As people approve the document, they stamp their *hanko*, or personal seal, on the document. Once the manager has indicated approval, the document may or may not continue up the line to the general manager, director, or president, depending on its importance. This method of document circulation is called *ringi seido*. While a long and time-consuming process, it does guarantee that once a proposal has been approved, all in the department have been fully briefed and consulted.

Changes in Management

The above discussion focused on the post-war system of Japanese management. The late 1990s, however, has seen this system fray a little around the edges. Lifetime employment and a seniority-based wage and promotion system are much easier to maintain when an economy is growing rapidly. As the economy slows down or stagnates, the employee profile for most companies will become top-heavy, necessitating the layoff of senior and middle managers. Many Japanese companies have also been moving production overseas to offset high domestic labor costs and to circumvent protectionist regulations and attitudes. This has resulted in loss of jobs at home. In 1998, unemployment in Japan reached its highest ever rate (between 4% and 5%) in decades. Job opportunities for younger Japanese men and women look much less promising than a decade ago when there were many jobs for each job seeker. In October 1998, according to the *Japan Times*, for every 100 people looking for work, there were only 48 job offers.

Company restructuring has so far attempted to deal with the need to layoff mid-career bureaucrats through early retirement and transfers to subsidiaries or other companies. In 1995, one-third of companies on the Tokyo Stock Exchange indicated that they were offering early retirement benefits to employees under 50 years of age, while 6% said that they were offering them to people under 40. Nippon Steel introduced a three-year restructuring plan in 1994 designed to eliminate 4,000 white collar (half through attrition and half through transfers to affiliate companies) and 3,000 blue collar jobs. Nonetheless, there have been many sad stories of employees in their forties and fifties who had devoted their entire working lives to a corporation and had expected that corporation to be committed to them only to be told their services were no longer needed.

Other changes include the increased acceptability of working for foreign companies. This bodes well for non-Japanese companies who have traditionally complained about the difficulty of finding good staff as most of those with options prefer to work for the large and famous Japanese corporations. Along with the prestige, part of the allure of those companies was the promise of long-term job security. As that diminishes, so does the risk of working for a foreign firm. Some companies have also begun recruiting throughout the year and according to need rather than in one annual intake. Even the age-wage promotion and pay system is being tinkered with as merit pay, rewarding employee performance, is being experimented with by companies such as Fujitsu. Young people are also much more interested in changing jobs than used to be the case. According to the Ministry of Labor, only 7% of those in the 15 to 24 age group and 5.5% in the 25 to 34 group expressed interest in changing jobs in 1971; by 1992, the figures had risen to about 19% and 15% respectively.

Some commentators argue that many parts of the system (from the role of the government discussed in chapter 2 to the forced high savings rates to lifetime employment), while suitable for a developing economy, make no sense for a developed one. In *Japan the System That Soured*, Richard Katz writes that

> "The ideas and strategies that worked so brilliantly in the era of industrial takeoff had outlived their usefulness once Japan's economy matured. And yet Japan could not bring itself to leave them behind. Over time, past strengths became the source of current weakness." (p 3)

What kind of path "will let Japan overcome its institutional roadblocks in the near future" and how long will it take, Katz wonders.

Others too wonder. Will the Japan that emerges look more Western? Some Japan hands, notably those based in the country, point to Japan's trade surplus, which as of December 1998 has been rising steadily for 19 months, and to Japan's $250 billion in foreign currency reserves and, as the world's largest creditor nation, an additional $1 trillion for emergencies and argue that the problems are not as dire as they are portrayed. They say that while the country is not without problems and that some change is inevitable in any country, Japan seems to do much that is right for itself, and there continues to be things from which we can learn. Whatever happens, the twenty-first century will be an interesting time to be an observer of Japan.

CHAPTER 4

The Challenge of Doing Business in Japan

No two business environments are the same. Just as there will be challenges to overcome when a company expands its business to another country, so will there be challenges when doing business in Japan. An essential element in any such strategy is knowledge— an awareness of personal and corporate attributes (Is your company up to the challenge?); an understanding of the market (Is Japan interested in what you want to sell?); and an appreciation of the unique characteristics of the Japanese business environment (How must the company adapt to suit Japanese conditions?).

See Things in Perspective

The Japanese business world is strong, vibrant, and highly motivated. Make sure you place the stories about current financial difficulties in their appropriate context. Take, for example, the recent climb in the national unemployment rate. At the end of 1998, Japan's unemployment rate had risen to the highest level since the 1950s. External critics clucked their disapproval and suggested that the bloom was off the Japanese economic rose. The United States, always anxious to assert its right to global economic pre-eminence, celebrated the fact that 1998 ended with one of the lowest national unemployment rates in a generation. One economy, the collective wisdom has it, is in near-recession, while the other is enjoying an unprecedented period of peacetime prosperity. Japan's 1998 unemployment rate had risen to 4.5%, while unemployment rate in the United States dropped to a low of 4.5%. (Critics say that Japan's unemployment rate is dramatically understated due to high levels of underemployment. On the other hand, the segments of U.S. society that no longer look for work are not included in official unemployment rates, thereby understating U.S. figures as well.) It is vital that Japan's economic performance—and its current difficulties—be kept in perspective.

The Japanese are highly sensitive about their country's economic performance and react quite strongly to external descriptions of their "crisis." They are particularly uneasy when foreign observers and politicians, most of whom are connected to economies that have performed more poorly than Japan for over 30 years, offer unsolicited advice and criticism of Japanese plans and actions. Even if the criticisms are on the mark—and Japan does have some serious problems to address—the Japanese do not take kindly to being reminded of the difficulties or to being told by non-Japanese people that they should adopt Western or North American solutions for their challenges.

A Dynamic Business Environment

So, let us start with a fairly basic point. The Japanese have a superb business environment—slightly different and, to foreigners, somewhat quirky. But they know how to do business. They operate in a world of limited contracts and relatively few legal conflicts (although the number has been growing in recent years). They have an immensely creative outlook on business and make extraordinary efforts to meet the needs of the world's most demanding consumers. Many of their corporate innovations, such as Edward Demming's "total quality management," were initially conceived by non-Japanese business people and have become world standards. The "just in time" delivery system perfected by the Japanese automobile and computer manufacturing sectors have spread around the globe. The Japanese model of labor-management relations have been adopted and implemented in many countries. (Many elements, such as the dormitory-style living expected of unmarried employees, do not transfer very well, particularly to

*In Japan, it is possible to find many different items in vending machines,
including beer, frozen meat, videos, and magazines.*

Western nations.) The Japanese are years ahead of most countries
in bringing advanced robotics onto the factory floor. On a broader
level, their reliance on individual responsibility and personal

contacts creates an interconnected and dependable network of business relationships.

Beware of observers who mock Japanese successes or who insist on a point-by-point comparison between foreign and Japanese business practices. The Japanese business system works for the Japanese and is designed to meet their needs. According to one recent report, only 8% of Japan's GDP is tied to external trade, the lowest of the major industrialized nations. This means, to put it simply, that Japan is quite self-contained economically. There is logic behind the nation's Japan-first commercial ethos.

There are some important differences between Japanese and Western corporations. Japanese business executives, for example, receive lower salaries than their Western counterparts. They are also likely to be far more loyal to their firms than the head office-jumping CEOs who lead many of the larger foreign firms. As we described in chapter 3, Japanese companies have a unique rhythm and logic that work extremely well for their country but makes little sense in other countries. Decisions can take longer and typically involve more people. Outsiders are often (and easily) frustrated by the delays. Avoid, if you can, the standard foreigners' assumption that Japanese business is inherently inefficient, unwieldy, or lacking in entrepreneurial drive. Japanese business, to put it simply, is Japanese. Most importantly, the Japanese business system works well and has produced many of the world's largest, most innovative, and most competitive international corporations. Mocking a system that has, in many ways, outstripped the rest of the world for over a quarter of a century suggests a narrowness of vision that needs to be overcome.

You should start from the premise that Japan works, that it works primarily for the Japanese, and that they are unlikely to make many concessions to suit the needs of the occasional foreign business person who seeks to enter the market. The responsibility to adapt, to change, and to learn rests with the outsider, not with a system that has consistently produced world-class results.

Recognize, too, that the challenges of doing business in Japan are not insurmountable. The Japanese are not as opposed to foreign participation as they were 15 years ago. Many foreign companies have materials for sale that are vital to Japanese business or that will find ready markets among Japanese consumers. If the right product or service is matched with the right attitude, the opportunities in Japan are considerable.

A Success Story
Roger Boisvert, a high-technology consultant working in Japan, realized the need for high-quality Internet service in the country. Japan lagged behind significantly in the development of the Internet, and the hidebound Japanese bureaucrats made few moves to liberalize the telecommunications sector. Boisvert recognized a tremendous opportunity, but he was wading into one of the most difficult, convoluted, and sensitive areas of Japanese business, one dominated by government regulations and a Byzantine commercial telecommunications network. His company, Global On-Line, started small, one of several thousand start-up Internet service providers, each locked into a localized market. With persistence, and an appreciation of the Japanese way of doing business, Boisvert carved out a market niche (high quality service at a premium price) and gradually developed a nationwide business. In the process, Global On-Line encouraged and required significant changes in government regulations and industry standards. What was once a small, struggling business has grown into a multi-million dollar enterprise that is on the cutting edge of the Asian Internet service sector.

What follows gives a brief overview of the major factors foreign businesses must take into account when setting up shop in Japan. Many of these issues will resurface in later chapters, as we suggest ways to deal with them. For now, the goal is to highlight potential problem areas and to indicate the nature of the challenges.

Important Factors to Consider

Quality

Japanese consumers, and therefore Japanese business people, are obsessed with quality standards. Slight deviations are not acceptable, and entire orders can (and have) been rejected on the basis of what most business people would consider to be minor imperfections. This applies across the board, from high-end products to inexpensive commodities. Products and services are expected to be delivered according to the standards set out in agreements or promised in promotional campaigns. Valuable business deals can easily collapse, often to the great annoyance of foreign traders who feel that the Japanese purchasers are unrealistic in their demands. One foreign flower producer was mortified to learn that a long-term contract had been voided by a Japanese supplier. A delivery that contained many thousands of specifically colored flowers included a handful of blossoms of the wrong color. To the exporter, the imperfections were minor and were left for the Japanese to sort out. They did—by canceling the contract. Similarly, a North American mining company had found a strong international niche by developing a mineral product of reasonable quality at a mid-price range. This approach to the market worked in dozens of countries but failed in Japan. Standards that apply in other countries will not necessarily work in Japan. In Japan, as the company executive noted, only the very best will do and for this a high price is paid.

Costs of Doing Business

Japan is an extremely expensive country, particularly for foreigners. The devaluation of the yen in 1997 and 1998 helped matters a little, but the truth is it costs a great deal of money to do business in Japan. Office space, particularly in Tokyo and other major centres, is very costly by the standards of most countries. The same is true of hotel accommodations, restaurant meals, domestic transportation, and even movie tickets! (Tickets cost two times more than in North America.) Salary costs are, by Western standards, quite high. The juxtaposition of high salaries and high costs means that, in comparative terms, Japanese workers are relatively well off by international standards. They benefit, especially when traveling abroad and capitalizing on the high exchange rate for the yen.

The costs of doing business in Japan present a formidable challenge, particularly for a small business. If you combine the economic realities with the Japanese expectation that foreign firms establish and maintain a domestic presence in order to "prove" their commitment to the Japanese market, cost alone can exclude a lot of foreign firms from competing successfully in the country. Many of Japan's leading trading partners—Australia, New Zealand, and Canada among them—have seen their currencies plunge relative to the yen over the past decade. The same exchange rate concerns mean that most countries have competitive advantages in regard to wages, energy costs, and general manufacturing expenses. It is here that the foreign firms find a tremendous opening relative to Japanese companies. But in order to capitalize on the opportunities, the foreign business needs to first make the contacts and establish a presence in Japan. For many, the costs of doing so are a hindrance, and the effort stops even before it begins.

Japan, however, need not be overly expensive. There are cheaper accommodations, such as "weekly mansions" (medium term lodgings) instead of hotels, and inexpensive yet excellent restaurants abound. There are ways of economizing on transportation and finding other ways to cut overall costs. These steps must be taken with caution. It is considered bad form to have a poor address, to take clients to a cheap restaurant, or to show signs of stinginess. Cost-cutting efforts must be taken with caution in order to ensure that potential Japanese partners do not get the wrong idea about the firm. It also takes considerable experience and knowledge to capitalize on the opportunity to economize.

Surviving the Red Tape and the Japanese Bureaucracy

Business people the world over complain about bureaucracy. Contrary to widespread opinion, even supposedly "open" economies such as the United States require attention to a bewildering array of regulations, duties, laws, and technical requirements. Japan is no different. But if you add to the standard business problem of the costs and time involved in managing red tape, the additional complexities of coping with a highly structured and overstaffed Japanese administrative service, a bigger challenge appears. The Japanese civil service is, first and foremost, Japanese. The dictates of lifetime employment that apply to the large corporations fit here as well. And working with people at the entry level positions—where most business contact is made—can be cumbersome and intensely bureaucratic. The language of commerce will, almost invariably be Japanese—expect few of the civil servants to be fluent in other languages—and this will add to the difficulties.

The challenge extends beyond matters of personnel and bureaucratic demeanor. In these two areas, Japan is no worse and often significantly better than most other countries. The real problem in dealing with the Japanese government is the baffling variety and complexity of its regulatory regimes. Japan has, for years, specialized in creating and protecting non-tariff barriers. Through the 1960s and 1970s, as Japanese products flooded world markets and generated vast trade surpluses, trading partners lobbied the Japanese to liberalize their economy and to provide access to foreign products. While some small concessions were made at the top level—tariffs and duties—little was done to the more complex regulatory systems. Products had to meet certain quality standards, had to be deemed suitable to Japanese consumers, and, most often, had to be approved through some little-known and hard-to-follow authorization process. The latter requirements could take months if not years, with no assurance of success.

Most observers linked the non-tariff barriers to inherent inefficiencies in the Japanese system of government. Others saw them for what they were—an important part of Japan's tactics for protecting local products and for keeping foreign businesses at bay. Many a foreign business, once enthusiastic about opportunities in Japan, gave up the game in disgust over the bureaucratic processes. Japan's more sincere trade liberalization, an integral part of the government's strategy for the past 15 years, has removed much of the regulatory overburden, but foreign companies still find the bureaucracy difficult to work with at times. Old habits, it seems, die hard, and the deeply inculcated desire to protect the Japanese market from outside forces remains in evidence.

No Cutting Corners

Most foreign business people would describe the Japanese as finicky. They are as concerned about details as they are about quality. Contracts and agreements will be examined very closely, itineraries will be checked, and hotel arrangements re-confirmed several times. The individual responsible for your company in a Japanese firm will call repeatedly to check on the progress of an order or a shipment. This individual will likely assume as much or more responsibility for something you failed to deliver. There will, conversely, be some irritation if reciprocal concern is not shown. This preoccupation with details extends throughout the business encounter. It matters, consequently, where people sit in business meetings, how they present their cards, what gifts are given, and how business arrangements are made.

In many other countries, business contacts and relationships are managed in a more casual fashion. There is greater latitude for change, a more relaxed attitude toward personal and professional relationships, and much less formality in the entire enterprise. Not so with the Japanese. Within the Japanese firm, form matters a great deal. And the details of individual contracts and business arrangements are deemed to be essential. To be casual about the details is to be casual about the relationship—a clear warning sign of a potentially unreliable partner. Take some solace from the fact that Japanese companies have had sufficient experience with non-Japanese firms that they do not react too strongly when their partner firms do not follow Japanese practices and standards. But realize, at the same time, that actions and failures to act are noted. Any firm wishing to establish a long-term, mutually beneficial relationship with Japanese companies had best learn to pay attention to the details. To do otherwise is to limit the attractiveness of your firm (or you personally), adding to the growing list of Japanese stories about insensitive, untrustworthy, and highly casual foreign business people.

The Japanese Distribution System

At times, it appears as if there is always one more hurdle, one final barrier, between the expense of start-up and profitability. More often than not, the barrier to foreign businesses is the distribution system. From a distance, there appears to be no reason for this to be a problem. Japan has a good transportation and communications infrastructure, and the relatively small size of the country should mean that moving supplies from the port of arrival to the market would proceed smoothly and efficiently. Not so. Consider Yoshikazu Takaishi's observation:

> "Japan has one of the most complex distribution systems in the world. This distribution system alone has been perceived by many foreign analysts and manufacturers to be the most significant barrier to penetrating the Japanese market. Distribution is responsible for providing roughly one out of six jobs in Japan, and provides nearly 15% of domestic production. The system is criticized for being inefficient and costly, in many cases adding nearly 50% to the price of the identical product sold outside of Japan."

— *The Business Guide to Japan*, p 221

This is hardly a ringing endorsement. The problem rests in two major areas: the multilayered nature of the distribution system and the keiretsu's operation of distribution companies.

With the exception of relationships between the largest wholesalers and the largest retailers, products generally follow a tortuous path between the factory and the retail outlet. Usually, the arrangement is as follows: factory, trading company, wholesaler, and a secondary wholesaler (and sometimes through four, five, or six other wholesalers) before being finally delivered to the shop. That most of Japan's hundreds of thousands of stores are small in size and operation mean that retailers rarely have much storage space of their own. As more than one observer has pointed out, Japan's primary warehouses appear to be the country's highways, which are perennially choked with hundreds of delivery trucks. Each step in the process adds more time and more costs. After being shipped from another country, moved through a Japanese port of entry, and finally to the distribution system, it is not surprising for the cost of a product to escalate to a point where it becomes non-economic.

At the other extreme, major manufacturers operate through closely connected distribution firms. They often sell directly to the public through stores that almost exclusively sell their products. While officially separate, the manufacturer and the distributor are partners and work together closely, not surprisingly, to the point where they ensure that a competitor's products are not carried by the same trucks or rail cars. Since the size and structure of the distribution firm is determined largely by the activities of the keiretsu manufacturing company (or companies), it is typically not looking for outside business. This arrangement is internally efficient and aids in the competition between manufacturers. It, however, adds to the inefficiency of the larger Japanese distribution system.

The foreign company moving into Japan is faced with something of a Hobson's Choice. It can opt for the general, wholesaler-based distribution system and put up with the inefficiencies, delays, and expenses of this arrangement. Or, even more expensively, it could contemplate setting up its own distribution system, an alternative that would deter all but the most ambitious entrant into the Japanese marketplace. This option has been used by a handful of foreign firms. A North American hair products company opted to sell directly to hair salons, to avoid the complex distribution system altogether. With much work and the careful cultivation of hair salon operators, the company was able to establish a profitable network to sell its products. The third, and most useful alternative, is to enter the market via some form of joint venture, pairing up with a Japanese manufacturer and thereby gaining access to his or her distribution system. This is most useful when bringing a brand new product into the market and less beneficial when seeking to compete directly with an existing Japanese product line.

Be careful, however, not to dismiss the Japanese distribution system as simply an inefficient vestige of an old, government-regulated sector. The distribution system carries some potentially great benefits. Distributors can often provide exceptional market intelligence, and through their sales and delivery workforce, they have direct access to hundreds, if not thousands, of stores on a regular basis. The feedback made possible by this system can prove to be valuable. Many warehouse operators focus specifically on one product or area, such as high fashion clothing. Connections with a well-established distributor provide access to their formidable market knowledge, sales force, and understanding of Japanese culture. The system, as well, allows the vast array of small, even the smallest, Japanese stores to carry a range of products that would not otherwise be possible, thus assisting with market penetration throughout the country.

The current system is under considerable pressure to change. The Japanese government has been encouraging the development of new firms to assist small and foreign firms with their efforts to break into the domestic market. Also, the growing complexity of the retail sector and the financial vulnerabilities of modern marketing are forcing the warehousing/distribution industry to drop some of the old ways, where personal relationships were of paramount importance in favor of higher priorities on service, delivery times, and costs. Warehouse operators have long accepted returns, one other way they protect small retail stores while encouraging them to take on new product lines; this practice is giving way to a more hard-nosed approach and a pay-on-delivery philosophy.

In most countries, delivery and distribution are relatively straightforward, competitive, customer-driven, and easily understood. In Japan, the distribution networks are complicated, expensive, and interventionist. Warehousing, delivery, and retail arrangements can be used by competitors to undercut newcomers and to keep foreign firms at bay. Recent changes are making Japanese distribution arrangements more user-friendly, but to an outsider observer, they remain obtuse and obstructionist. Tread carefully.

Knowing Your Japanese Consumers

The headstrong race toward economic globalization has left many companies with the impression that products and services are easily transportable around the world. There is much truth to this, even in Japan. Major brand names carry tremendous cachet in Japan, and consumers are willing to pay substantial premiums to gain access to widely recognized products. And the rapid expansion of Western products into the farthest corners of the globe make it easy to understand why companies expect Japanese consumers to respond similarly to their wares. While this can happen—McDonald's (with a Japanese twist or two) is commonplace in the country—the Japanese market retains a variety of unique elements.

Any company hoping to do well in Japan had best spend some time learning Japanese customs, tastes, and expectations. We have

Asakusa in Tokyo is a "temple town" and provides Japanese and visitors alike with a good experience of traditional Japanese culture.

already mentioned the Japanese obsession with quality and the premium they are often prepared to pay to get the "best" product. At the other end, there are some quirky elements. Clothing with bizarre English phrases are very popular. The phrases include sentence fragments, illogical connections, and somewhat silly references. But they sell well.

In the middle are a variety of other patterns worth considering: the Japanese enthusiasm for personalized items, the priority given to small items (due to the size of apartments and houses), and fascination with communication devices and consumer electronics. Customers expect that great care will be taken with packaging and wrapping. They will, moreover, expect the very best gear and equipment, even if these things vastly exceed their requirements. Buyers of golfing, skiing, or fishing equipment will typically buy the best supplies and will insist on the "full" package. One of the most intriguing images in recent years was watching a fully equipped Japanese fly-fisherman practicing his casting—atop a ten-story apartment complex in Tokyo. On the food front, the Japanese are quite selective and are far from slavish in their response to imported foodstuffs.

Japanese consumers are excellent buyers. They expect top quality and are prepared to pay for it. They will experiment with new products, Japanese or imported, and they can be enticed, through advertising and promotion, to give new items a shot. Japanese companies and an increasing number of foreign firms have learned how to cultivate this market and to provide both the quality and variety expected by consumers. But, if you are new to the country, expect the unexpected, and be prepared to be flexible.

One other point worth noting is that women are responsible for most of the purchases in Japan. Generally, men work very long hours and have little time for shopping. In most families—and even after they have begun to make inroads into the regular workforce—women are responsible for managing the finances of the family. Not surprisingly, therefore, Japanese companies devote a great deal of energy and effort toward cultivating the support and loyalty of female consumers. Given that they control the purse strings, this is a wise business practice.

Serving Your Japanese Consumers

Japanese consumers pride themselves on their loyalty and expect the same in return. While they can be demanding, finicky, and, in the first instance, quite difficult to bring on board, they can also be determined, supportive, and your best advertising medium. To the average Japanese consumer, a commercial relationship is akin to a personal one (particularly if there is a high cost item involved). They expect strong service during and, especially, after the sale. They expect to have any defects dealt with promptly—and without an argument (apologies are expected and are given readily). And they anticipate that the store will endeavor to ensure that their products work well and are serviced promptly and as required. You can go "down-scale" in Japan. In many shopping districts, you can find discount houses or even firms selling out of unfurnished quarters. Customers who venture into these stores know and accept the risks involved. More generally, however, after-sales service to the distributor, retailer, and customer is essential to the successful placement of a new product.

It is not easy to do business in Japan. And there are no assurances, in Japan or any place for that matter, that money spent on entering a new market will result in corporate profits. While many companies have flourished in Japan, others have failed and failed miserably. These caveats aside, the Japanese market presents some formidable challenges, most of them rooted in the national culture and the lingering legacy of decades of protectionism. The marketplace is complex and multifaceted, and the intricacies of establishing and maintaining a business can deter even the most committed business person. When the nuances of bureaucracy and regulations are added to the uniqueness in marketing strategies, customer expectations, and distribution systems, the Japanese economy appears difficult and uncompromising.

While this was substantially true in the past, when only the newer, larger, and well-financed international corporations had the time and money to try to break into Japan, the situation is improving with each passing year. The Japanese business environment is opening up due to government fiat, greater Japanese experience with foreign businesses, and consumer interest in international products. Regulations are being streamlined, distribution systems being made more competitive, and access to consumers improving. As more Japanese travel internationally, their taste for foreign goods grows, and their interest in international brand gains momentum. Remember, too, that Japan is a solid middle class nation. The majority of its population is well off, with considerable disposable income. As a consequence, consumers are ready and able to experiment with new products and to try out new services. Formidable though the challenges may be to doing business in Japan, the opportunities are very real, and the commercial potential for international firms remains substantially untapped.

CHAPTER 5

Setting Up a Business in Japan

Do Market Research

No wise corporation undertakes international expansion on a whim. The decision to move into Japan or any country should be made on the basis of careful market analysis, extensive local research, frequent meetings with government and business representatives, and a detailed consideration of the costs and benefits of the venture. Fanciful accounts of the wealth and opportunities in Japan mean nothing if the decision to enter the country creates a financial nightmare for a firm. In Japan, and elsewhere, there are no guarantees. The market contains almost as many pitfalls as opportunities. Every success story can be matched with at least one account of a failure.

The best advice is to approach Japan with a healthy mix of optimism and caution. Look for long-term opportunities and beware of short-term barriers. Bankrupt companies are not around to share in the benefits of long-term prosperity. The legal and technical issues are often seen as less interesting than initial market research, product development, and preliminary business planning. But it is here, in the nuts and bolts of commercial operations, that your firm will confront the reality of Japan—warts, blemishes, smiles, and good wishes together—and its business environment. A careful approach in the first instance will auger well for the long term. Even the decision not to proceed at this time, or with this product, might well be in the company's best interests, laying the foundation for a more profitable entry at a later time. Standard rules of business apply in Japan—it is the nuances and details that differ. In this chapter, we will examine several major issues that a firm should consider before proceeding too far down the path of setting up shop in Japan.

Modes of Entry into the Japanese Market

Your company is interested in moving into the Japanese market and is considering the next step in the process. You have before you the standard options.

Using a Commercial Agent

Most companies are dissuaded from moving directly into Japan and opt instead to work through a commercial agent. There are hundreds of import/export firms in the country, many of the them with top-notch reputations for reliability, successful product placement, and responsiveness to clients' needs. Smaller firms, in particular, find that agents are particularly useful in establishing a market for their products. They provide immediate access, years of direct experience, extensive local knowledge and contacts, market research, a regional or national sales force, and, because the relationship stands to be mutually beneficial, useful advice on product placement and advertising.

Franchising

For certain companies and service providers, franchising presents an attractive alternative. Western brand names carry considerable market potential in Japan, and the franchise system can capitalize on this attraction. It also means that the challenges of coping with local regulations and customs fall to the franchisee, almost certainly a Japanese individual. The franchise operation has enjoyed considerable success, as seen by the long-standing presence of McDonald's and Kentucky Fried Chicken in Japan, and the more recent introduction (to huge crowds) of Starbucks coffee shops.

Direct Marketing

New technologies, particularly the Internet and telephone call centres, combined with the long-standing Japanese interest in catalogue shopping and door-to-door sales, have developed fertile ground for direct marketing. Exercise caution, however, as Japanese consumers are just as demanding as consumers in the West about quality and service from direct marketing firms and specialty shops. Direct marketing should not be seen as a means of "sneaking" second-rank merchandise into the hands of unsuspecting Japanese consumers. Bear in mind that Japanese consumers are often reluctant to deal directly with distributors based outside the country (the record for service and reliability is not particularly strong), and prefer to address their orders and inquiries to a Japan-based contact.

Licensing

Companies looking for a way to break into the market with minimal direct investment often attempt to license their product to a Japanese manufacturing company. The national manufacturing is vast and complicated, ranging in size from the huge keiretsu conglomerates to tiny backroom, mom-and-pop assembly shops. It is often possible to find a Japanese firm interested in taking on a foreign product. Such a company would have its own distribution connections and the local contacts necessary to bring the product to market quickly. There are reasons to be cautious with licensing arrangements. In the past, several of the larger Japanese firms have signed licensing agreements with small, innovative foreign companies, who then discover that the Japanese partner is in no rush to bring the product or service to the market. Indeed, in extreme cases, the Japanese business sat on the technology until their in-house product was ready for market. If you are considering such an arrangement, opt for small to medium-sized Japanese firms and larger companies, as well as investigate carefully the Japanese company's reasons for interest in your product.

Joint Ventures

Joint ventures provide an excellent means of initial entry, perhaps the most popular—and often the most successful—means of entering the Japanese market. This arrangement is best suited to companies that wish to establish a long-term presence in Japan but are concerned about the initial costs and complications of market entry. With the right joint venture partner, the foreign firm gains access to local contacts and distribution arrangements, as well as local market intelligence and experience.

Choosing a Commercial Partner

Once you have investigated the Japanese market and have determined that there is considerable potential for your firm, you then face the most crucial decision of all. How serious are you about doing business in Japan? Being realistic is the key here. Calculate the costs and difficulties involved in setting up operations in Japan. The decision should not be undertaken unless you are confident that your firm will maintain a long-term presence in the country. (The Japanese have seen hundreds of foreign firms come and go, and do not consider a international company to be part of the local scene until they have been around for quite a few years.) It may be in your firm's best interests to simply work through a distributor and to respond to orders for your product. Start-up costs are minimal and, although potential returns are reduced, the Japan-based distributor looks after all the local and cultural considerations. It is worth spending a great deal of time with this very basic decision; your company's future in Japan might well depend on the appropriateness of your choice.

If you have decided to proceed with a Japan-based partner, a separate set of considerations kicks in. Selecting a commercial partner requires great care and due diligence. There are numerous ways of checking out the bona fides of a trading company or potential joint venture partner. Your national embassy is usually an excellent first point of contact, although the company's utility will be partially dependent on the size and complexity of its Japan operations. Professional and trade associations can provide useful market intelligence, as can foreign chambers of commerce and other business organizations. There are several other considerations to keep in mind. Check the agent's regional reach. Do they sell only in the Tokyo region or do they distribute products throughout the country? You should also check out their track record with other foreign firms, the reliability record for handling distribution, and marketing strategies and programs. Also, beware of the voracious appetites of the larger corporations. Creative, smaller firms, particularly in fast-moving high-technology and software fields, have often been absorbed by their larger partner. It helps to check out your potential partner's track record on this account. Rest assured, by the way, that they will be checking you out even more thoroughly. The Japanese preoccupation with detail and research is nowhere better evident than in the lead-up to partnership or joint venture discussions.

Contracts and Formal Agreements

Japanese business people do not place a lot of faith in legal contracts and consequently do not devote a great deal of time negotiating highly detailed agreements. Their priority, is on cultivating a mutually beneficial relationship, not on "besting" a trading partner in a contract struggle. Two observers note that

> "[T]he Japanese rely more on human relationships than the law or legal rights and obligations. The key element of the human relationship which the Japanese sees in the contractual relations is trust (*shinrai kankei*). The most important thing for Japanese business people is to earn the trust of the other party ... [Y]ou cannot spent too much energy and time in order to earn the trust of potential customers."
>
> — *The Business Guide to Japan*, p 91

Many Western business people seek the security of signed contracts, sometimes even losing potentially valuable business deals by worrying excessively over the fine points of contracts.

Most foreign companies interested in doing business in Japan will only go part way down the path. In the majority of cases, making arrangements with a distributor or licensing a product or service will meet company objectives and fit within available resources. Occasionally, joint venture operations will be suitable; in most such instances, the foreign company brings technology, a product, and/or capital to the table, leaving the Japanese firm to provide the local expertise needed to succeed. For a small number of firms, the logical step is to establish a formal presence in Japan, either by way of a small sales and marketing office or, more dramatically, by opening a production line. If your firm opts for the latter options, ensure that you secure good, professional advice. You can usually get very good assistance from your country's embassy in Japan, and they in turn can provide you with contacts to consultants and advisors.

Japan is a very tricky administrative environment, and there are layers upon layers of regulations and issues that have to be addressed. Hiring local expertise, even if only on a short-term basis, is usually strongly advised; to proceed on your own has the potential to create numerous difficulties and could result in a great deal of wasted time and effort.

Taxes and Related Regulations

Japanese taxes and tax regulations are complicated—hardly a surprising discovery. Foreign business people looking to set up shop in Japan should consult a local expert before proceeding. The Japanese financial controversy has resulted in pressures to change some of the regulatory and tax systems, so Japanese tax law is likely to be more dynamic than usual in the coming years. (For a useful overview of the Japanese tax system, refer to W. Temple Jorden, "The Japanese Tax System," in *The Business Guide to Japan*.) The general overview is as follows: individual income tax rates are relatively high by international standards, although a wide range of deductions is permitted. Non-residents are taxed only on income earned in Japan. Corporations are subject to a corporate tax, a withholding tax, and local taxes.

Companies may face combined corporate and local taxes in the range of 50%. Japan maintains a fairly strong system of taxation on gifts and inheritances, and aggressively goes after companies and individuals who shelter their income in tax havens. Japan also has a sizable consumption (or value-added) tax, currently set at 5%. Further, the country maintains a wide array of other taxes, including property taxes, stamp taxes, transaction taxes, and other such duties.

In addition to a fairly extensive tax regime, Japan maintains an extensive series of regulations and standards that have a direct impact on business. Most of these are in accordance with international laws and conventions, including regulations governing patents and copyright, product liability, and intellectual property rights. Some of the regulations, such as those governing trademark protection, are less decisive and clear and might cause problems for some companies. In the past, Japan used a complex set of product standards that required foreign firms to suffer through a lengthy product review process before the item was cleared for domestic sale. Often times, the cost and delays involved convinced the foreign companies to abandon their efforts to break into the Japanese market—the government's implicit goal from the beginning. The greater openness of the contemporary Japanese market means that many of these regulatory procedures have been somewhat relaxed, but problems can still occur.

Lawyers and the Law

Japanese business functions with a surprisingly small number of lawyers—something the Japanese point to with considerable pride. The small number of lawyers in the country (only a tiny percentage of candidates pass the nation's law examinations) and restrictions on their employment by foreign firms means that it is generally difficult for a foreign company to secure Japanese legal advice.

The Japanese court system is not particularly "user-friendly," and seeking redress for contractual and business matters through civil courts is generally neither cost-effective nor efficient. *Bengoshi*, or Japanese lawyers, charge very high rates and often require up-front payments for potentially lengthy cases.

Most companies settle legal controversies out of court, a process that receives strong encouragement from both the courts and the government. Settlements, rather than "win-lose" court battles, fit in with the Japanese desire for harmony and their wish to avoid legal conflict. In fact, most business matters in Japan are settled before court proceedings commence; it is seen as a highly aggressive move to start legal proceedings, and most firms will seek a negotiated settlement rather than go to court. The cumbersome, overworked, and incredibly slow Japanese legal system then (sort of) kicks into gear. Resolution of business conflicts in the courts can easily take many years.

Financing Japanese Operations

Japan is one of the world's richest countries, with the highest savings rate and vast monetary reserves. At the same time, Japan's financial markets have been historically rigid and inflexible, and have not been well-adapted to the needs of foreign businesses based in the country. Loans were generally made only against property—a good bet in the years of the bubble economy and a risky gamble thereafter—and commercial credit was hard to locate. The current financial crisis in Japan has only made banks and other financial institutions more cautious, resulting in the withdrawal of credit from even healthy businesses, which have often forced clearly unnecessary bankruptcies in the process. A good number of foreign companies, unable to find a sympathetic ear among Japanese bankers, have looked elsewhere for their funding. With government encouragement, the situation has eased a little as a result of banking reforms introduced in 1997 and 1998, but the arrangements are far from being flexible or readily accessible.

There are other ways to raise capital, beyond funding the Japanese operation directly out of corporate revenues. The Japanese government itself has been an increasingly important source of funds for foreign businesses, particularly those promising to develop high-employment projects. Do not expect the generous subsidies that can be found in other countries. Japanese authorities simply do not see the need to go after foreign business in this fashion. Many foreign companies use funds from banks and financial institutions in their home country, and find these domestic lenders to be much easier and faster to deal with than their Japanese counterparts. Even more common is the use of funds from a joint venture partner. Generally, a foreign firm brings a specific product or expertise into a joint venture, while the Japanese firm offers money and Japan-specific knowledge.

The Japanese financial system has long been seen as one of the more significant barriers to economic development, and this has been particularly true for foreign-owned corporations. The recent series of financial scandals and disasters has only made the situation worse, and increased dissatisfaction with the limited flexibility and restricted range of services in the banking sector. While the government continues to promise sweeping reforms, only relatively minor changes have been made to date. For now, foreign firms wishing to do business in Japan will have to look to sources other than Japanese banks for financial backing.

Expatriate Staff

Just as local staff are vital to any company's operations in Japan, so too are the expatriate staff brought in. These individuals provide a pivotal link between Japan and the home country, and for the most part serve as cultural and commercial interpreters. The standard approach to bringing overseas workers to Japan is to treat the country as something of a "hardship" posting and to thus provide a variety of compensations. These involve very spacious living quarters (typically much larger than those that local staff can afford), trips home and other financial benefits. The treatment of expatriate staff often becomes a matter of concern and tension within the Japanese offices of foreign companies, if only because of the significant benefits given to an individual who might be less than useful in the Japanese setting. The pattern of overcompensating foreign workers has the effect of convincing them that they are indeed hard done by and deserve the extra perks and salary. This is not an effective long-term strategy. Companies are well-advised, within reasonable limits, to compensate foreign workers similarly and to avoid the temptation to reproduce domestic living conditions (at prohibitive cost) in Japan. For employees to be truly successful in Japan, they should be prepared to work in the country on Japan's terms.

Many firms address these challenges by endeavoring to hire non-Japanese people who are already in Japan. In such instances, concerns about adaptation, the extra costs of recruitment and initial establishment, issues of adjustment and acculturation, and related matters are dealt with early on. Not surprisingly, the practice of "raiding" expatriate workers is widespread in Japan, so do not be surprised if several of your prized employees are recruited away in fairly short order.

Labor Laws

Foreign firms working in Japan will invariably rely heavily on Japanese employees. They will, in turn, be the eyes and ears of the company in Japan, providing valuable market and commercial intelligence. Time and time again, international firms have identified their local staff as being essential to their success (or failure). As a consequence, it is vital that employees be treated well and that they be managed as per Japanese law. It is worth noting, as a starting point, that Japanese law does not outlaw discrimination. You can hire women or men, specifying age and a variety of physical characteristics. Most Japanese employers request that a photograph be attached to an application and use the photograph in their selection processes.

Japan has a strong and complex labor law, which is better on description of actions to be avoided than on the identification of specific penalties to be imposed on offending firms. The Labor Standards Law sets out the minimal requirements for the workplace and provides a useful guide for the management of the workplace. Companies are expected to provide the standard array of benefits to employees, including retirement allowances, holiday pay, and the like. Each firm is expected to develop a set of "Work Rules" and to have them vetted by the local Labor Standards Office. Japanese companies have an enviable record of labour-management relations, one that is based on mutual respect and employee involvement in the affairs of the company concerned. Most Japanese firms have company unions or employee association, which are effectively a branch of the firm and not a separate trade union (as Westerners would understand the term). Larger foreign firms might well find that they are attractive candidates for the still-active trade union movement.

Other Considerations

Once the decision has been made to set up an office in Japan, a thousand smaller details emerge. Where should the office be placed? What is reasonable price for rent? What costs should be covered for expatriate staff brought to Japan? How many local employees should be hired? You should note that, between JETRO (Japan External Trade Organization) and some of the major embassies in Japan, there are a variety of short-term business support centres that provide office space and even secretarial help for firms setting up shop in Japan. This is often a very good way to get started in the country. The following identifies other major considerations:

Staff

Most observers and business people argue that finding the right staff is essential for business success. Several factors contribute to a complicated Japanese business environment, such as the difficulty of locating suitable Japan-based personnel, including Japanese people, and the time and costs involved in bringing someone in from the home country. Perhaps the best advice, especially for those seeking to establish a sizable office, is to hire a trained and experienced office manager or human resource manager. This individual can help address the many practical and technical questions involved in staff matters and can prove to be instrumental in getting the business office open on a proper footing.

Office

Selecting a proper office site is a difficult task, particularly given the exceptionally high rates charged in major Japanese cities. The primary considerations in picking a location are proximity to a major train or subway line, access to business partners and financial offices, availability of suitable accommodations in the vicinity for overseas visitors, and availability of services and restaurants. Check to ensure the building is wired for contemporary technology; selecting the wrong building can require extensive outfitting costs to provide the firm with appropriate computer access.

Office Design

The Japanese favor an open-office design, believing that it facilitates office communication and decision making. Westerners' desire for closed offices is seen as unfriendly and inefficient.

Lease and Contract Terms

The recent slow down in the Japanese economy has created considerable opportunities for new businesses. Lease arrangements, which only recently bordered on the ridiculous, have become more favorable. Deposits of two to three years rent have been reduced to a more reasonable three to six months. In Japan, tenant protection is very strong, provided rent has been paid, so the prospect of losing a suitable location is relatively minimal.

Selecting a Site: Is there Business Life Beyond Tokyo?

One of the most common mistakes that foreign firms make in approaching Japan is to equate Tokyo with the country as a whole. Tokyo is a vibrant, powerful, and well-connected business centre. It is truly one of the world's greatest cities. But the country has numerous other cities—Osaka, Sapporo, Sendai, Kobe, Kyoto, Hiroshima, and Nagasaki—that are deserving of attention. International airline connections with these cities continue to improve, and each is the centre of a sizable and wealthy regional economy. There are many advantages to being in other cities, such as lower costs, less foreign competition, strong local enthusiasm for improving international trade connections, and relatively untapped markets. Local governments are particularly eager to attract additional business away from the main metropolitan area—there are strong pools of anti-Tokyo sentiment throughout the country—and foreign businesses are likely to receive strong encouragement and assistance from local authorities.

There is something of a herd mentality in the foreign business community. Facilities and services for non-Japanese people are much better developed in Tokyo than in most other places (with the possible exception of Okinawa, which has a very large American military base nearby), and expatriates requiring schooling, professional assistance, Western products and restaurants, and a well-functioning round of foreign social engagements will find these and more in Tokyo. It is, however, because of this concentration of foreign business people in Tokyo that firms are well-advised to at least consider setting up shop in other centres.

The brief description provided above is far from being a comprehensive guide to the intricacies of establishing a presence in Japan. Most foreign companies opt to move slowly and to proceed initially through a distribution agreement or some other limited business engagement. For companies that are more serious about entering the Japanese market, the joint venture has emerged as the most common means of extending operations into the country. Only a relatively small number of firms go so far as to even set up a representative office, let alone production facilities, in Japan, a reflection both of the difficulties of establishing and maintaining a presence in the country and of foreign reluctance to commit very significant resources to the Japanese market. Those firms that decide to take the leap of faith into Japan quickly discover that the cultural complexities of the country are more than replicated at the commercial, governmental, and personal level. That the process is difficult does not mean that it should be avoided. Some very successful foreign business ventures have taken root in Japan. The significant step of establishing a commercial operation in Japan should come only after careful review of the market and the long-term possibilities of growth in the country.

CHAPTER 6

The Rituals of Business

Japanese society is formal. There are appropriate ways to behave in almost every social situation. There are set greetings when leaving or returning home and correct ways to accept a gift or decline a compliment. The Japanese recognize correct ways to accept a gift or decline a compliment. The Japanese have ritualized sayings for funerals and appropriate clothing for specific situations. (Schoolchildren wear uniforms, and even novice skiers are expected to have snazzy ski clothes.) Japanese arts, from the tea ceremony to judo, emphasize the importance of learning the proper way to perform each and every tiny step that makes up the art. Students perform endless repetitions of these movements until they become second nature. *Rei*, or form, underpins Japanese society; the literal meaning of the Japanese word for excuse me is *shitsurei*, or to lose form, as to lose form is considered rude. Rituals and order are the social lubricants that help Japanese society function smoothly.

That there are appropriate ways to behave in business situations then comes as no surprise. Rituals and protocols ensure that everyone is comfortable. Knowing a little about the way business is conducted Japanese-style can benefit both you and your Japanese counterparts.

First Contacts and the Use of Introductions
Business relations in Japan tend to be based on trust and are usually entered into slowly and with a view to the long term. For this reason, the Japanese do not tend to respond well to cold calls. To approach a Japanese businessman without an introduction from an intermediary would not only be unwise, it would probably also be unproductive. A cold call would be unlikely to even get a

Spirituality remains a very important part of Japanese life. At a shrine in Takayama, Japanese businessmen pray for a prosperous New Year.

meeting arranged. To have an introduction from a mutual friend or business colleague would be the best route to arranging a first meeting, but as a last resort, an introduction from your embassy would probably be effective. It would be best if a meeting was arranged so that the introduction could occur in person, but if this is not possible, then a letter of introduction would be appropriate. Connections are vital in Japan, and it would be wise to begin cultivating connections long before you actually go to Japan. Local Japan friendship societies would be a good place to start.

Introductions are imbued with a great deal of importance in Japan. People do not introduce other people lightly as the person who does the introduction takes some responsibility for the future of the relationship. The Japanese feel obliged to meet someone introduced by a friend or business acquaintance so the person performing the introduction is putting himself or herself on the line. If someone introduces you, you must not only express your gratitude but ensure that you do nothing to discredit your *shookai-sha*, or "introducer."

Business Cards

Business cards in Japan convey much more than identification and information for future contact Details of the card owner's position and company are vital indicators of status and hierarchy. Business cards are exchanged frequently at all first meetings with a significant degree of formality.

Bring as many *meishi* , or business cards, with you on your business trips to Japan. Have your business cards translated into Japanese on one side. Think carefully about how your title will translate into the Japanese hierarchy, and see if your position can match one of the traditional Japanese titles (see table on managerial titles). Never leave your accommodations or hotel without your meishi as you never know when you might meet someone with

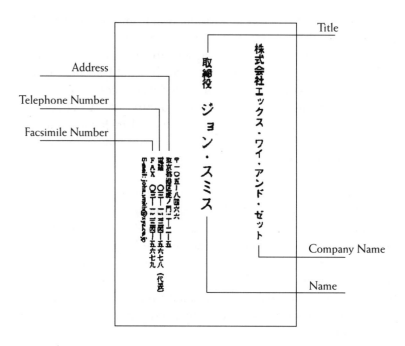

Title

Address

Telephone Number

Facsimile Number

Company Name

Name

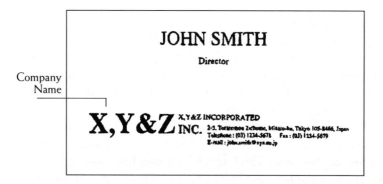

Company Name

JOHN SMITH

Director

An example of a Japanese business card. Source: Jetro Marketing Series, Doing Business in Japan (Japan: JETRO, 1998), p 19.

whom you will need to exchange cards. It is worth buying a holder in which to keep both your business cards and the ones you will receive. It is not acceptable to stuff them in your wallet or in a pocket. If you are unable to find a business cardholder at home, you can buy them in Japan at any stationery store. Keep your card holder in your front inside pocket (for men) or in your purse for women. Never keep it in the rear seat pocket as this is considered rude.

You should stand when you give and receive business cards. If possible, give your card out carefully and with both hands. Do not deal your cards out as if you are playing poker! Exchange cards with one person at a time. Turn the card to face the person to whom you are giving it. So, if your card has been translated, have the Japanese side face up, and turn it so that the writing faces the recipient. This makes it easier for the person receiving your card to read it. Receive the other person's card with both hands, and spend some time reading the card. As people exchange cards, they say out their names and their company names, and express pleasure at meeting the other party.

In case you did not catch the other person's name, you can confirm it by reading the card. This is the time to ensure that you are comfortable with the pronunciation of the other person's name. For instance, you can clarify by asking, "Ah, it is Mr. Tanaka, isn't it?" The Japanese also do this as Japanese characters can often be read in more than one way, and sometimes, it can be particularly difficult with names to be sure which is the correct pronunciation. You might also want to make a mental note of the person's title, department, and company. (You can compare the Japanese title on the card with the list of managerial titles to make sure the translation is accurate.) Asking a question about the person's company or the department is also welcome at this time. This is the first stage of the relationship so showing knowledge of or interest in the person or the company is naturally well received. Don't put the card away too soon.

Exchanging business cards is done with care in Japan. Cards are seen as an extension of the person, and so handling them casually or carelessly is insulting to the other person. After receiving a person's card, carefully place it in your business cardholder. At a meeting, it is also acceptable to lay the cards you have received out in front of you, matching their locations with the persons from whom you received the cards. This can help you keep names and titles straight.

Forms of Address

As mentioned, when the Japanese meet in business settings, they introduce themselves by saying the name of their company and their name (usually in that order). The English equivalent would be something such as "I'm ABC company's Mr Smith." This is followed by the Japanese equivalent of "It is nice to meet you," and a common expression that does not translate easily into English but expresses the desire for a good future relationship. (See chapter 9 for this and other useful expressions.)

First names are rarely used in Japan. The Japanese usually call each other by their last names and attach the suffix *san*, which means "Mr." "Mrs.," or "Ms." Many Japanese would therefore be surprised if you were to address them by their first name and suggest that they call you by yours. If your Japanese counterparts have spent time abroad, they could well have picked up either English nicknames or a shortened version of their first names. Unless a Japanese person suggests that you use his or her first name, it is better not to do so.

For teachers, doctors, and company executives, the Japanese often use those titles in place of the person's name. This is an indication of respect and occurs even outside of business. So, people use *sensei* when addressing teachers and doctors and *kacho* when talking to the company manager and *okusan* when speaking to someone's wife. You should, however, only do this once you have gained some degree of familiarity with the people concerned.

In most cases, you will be calling someone by their last name with the suffix san (e.g. Tanaka-san). San is a mark of respect, an honorific in linguistic terms, and is therefore not to be used with your own name. When introducing yourself, you simply state your last name and the name of your company.

Status and Rank within a Japanese Company

The Japanese business world is very hierarchical. All employees of a company will know who joined when. Those who join in one year form a class or *dooki* (same period), and members of this class stay closely in step in both rank and salary for at least the first decade or two of their careers. As most companies put their new employees through a relatively rigorous training period at the outset of their employment, strong relationships are often formed with others in one's dooki. As new recruits undergo training in various positions and transfer among departments throughout their careers, these contacts prove very useful.

For the Japanese employee, outside of those in one's dooki, all other company employees are either senior or junior to him or her. Those who joined the company earlier (incidentally, this is also the case for school classes, clubs, and teams), are referred to as *senpai*, or senior, superior, or elder, by those who joined later. A senpai looks out for and acts as the mentor for his or her *kohai*, or junior, who in return respects and obeys the senpai. While some senpai-kohai relationships are closer than others, the general pattern of the senior person commanding respect and giving instruction while the younger employee obeys is common. This relative hierarchy among employees, therefore, affects every aspect of the interaction between senior and junior employees, from the language used (forms of address, verb endings, and even verbs themselves change depending on the person addressed and the person speaking) to appropriate seating arrangements (the more senior person sits down first and usually in the center seat) to who pays at a restaurant (the more senior person).

While there are variations among companies depending on their size and structure, there is a general corporate hierarchy through which all Japanese male employees (and sometimes some female employees) progress. The table below outlines the main managerial titles and their English equivalents. Japanese employees will address those at ranks above that of *shaiin*, or employee, by their titles. While the variety of titles might be a little confusing to a foreigner, they are functional and identify the status of the individual.

A Typical Ranking System in a Japanese Company

Kaichoo	會長	Chairman
Shachoo	社長	President
Fuku-shachoo	副社長	Executive Vice President
Senmu Torishimariyaku	専務取締役	Executive Managing Director
Joomu Torishimariyaku	常務取締役	Managing Director
Torishimariyaku	取締役	Director
Buchoo	部長	General Manager
Kachoo/Buchoo Dairi	課長／部長代理	Manager/Acting General Manager
Kakarichoo/Kachoo Dairi	係長／課長代理	Group Chief/Acting Manager
Buin/Kain	部員／課員	Staff

Source: Association for Japanese-Language Teaching, *Japanese for Busy People* (Kodansha International).

Note that the hierarchical order is not always consistent. Sometimes, for example, jichoo is above buchoo, and sometimes it is below. The English translations can also be misleading and should used only as a general guide.

As hierarchy is important to the Japanese business person, it is important for those who want to do business with the Japanese to respect and understand its significance. Pay attention to the interactions among your Japanese counterparts, read business cards carefully, try to ascertain who is the most senior, and accord that person the requisite level of respect.

By the same token, recognize that if the Japanese are hosting you, they will also want to know who is the most senior in your group so that they can treat that person with the respect his or her rank warrants. Uncomfortableness with hierarchy among some Westerners often leads to attempts to avoid signaling someone out for special treatment. In Asia, status and hierarchy matter, and not paying attention to levels of status can have disastrous consequences. In *When Business East Meets Business West*, Christopher Engholm describes an American delegations' visit to Taiwan. The Taiwanese hosts rented a limousine for the CEO and a van for the rest of the group. The Americans decided that everyone should get a chance to ride in the limo so they rotated leaders. The Taiwanese were very offended and considered such frivolity in bad taste. The Japanese would react in a similar fashion. So, if you are a guest in Japan or almost anywhere in Asia, follow the lead of your host. Do not fight the hierarchy and formality that permeate Japanese society, but work within it.

The First Meeting

The Japanese emphasis on trusting business relationships means that at the first meeting with a potential new business associate the purpose will be to get to know each other. The Japanese will be endeavoring to determine if you are sincere, trustworthy, and interested in committing to a long-term relationship with their company. At the first meeting and perhaps even the first few meetings, the Japanese will not be interested in talking much about business. They will be more concerned about getting to know you. Any business conversation that takes place will probably be a sharing of information about the two companies' corporate philosophies, general plans, organizational structure, and the like. The rest of the conversation will probably focus on general topics such as the weather, golf, baseball, hobbies, their visits to your country, and your impressions of Japan. If you know a little about recent events in Japan (read a Japanese newspaper upon arrival), this interest is always well received.

Dressing for Business

The best rule of thumb for business meetings in Japan is to dress conservatively. For men, a dark suit with a fairly subdued tie is best. A stroll around the business district of any Japanese city will reveal large numbers of Japanese business men in very similar dark-colored suits. It would be unusual to find a Japanese business man in any other outfit. Women should also stick to outfits that are reasonably conservative in color and style. Avoid low-cut or tight blouses or dresses. Bright colors, such as red, are also not recommended. A simple dark skirt and blazer would be a good bet. As you could well end up sitting on a *tatami* floor (in a Japanese style restaurant, for example), it will be more comfortable and relaxing if your skirt is not too short. Along the same lines, you could well end up having to take off your shoes so check to make sure there are no holes in your socks or stockings! Avoid heavy makeup, perfume, and ostentatious jewelry.

As Japanese summers can be very hot and humid, wear short-sleeved shirts and light weight clothing, but men should still wear (or at least bring along) a lightweight suit jacket. It would also be worth carrying a handkerchief to dry your face when the weather becomes humid. (Actually, it is a good idea to carry a handkerchief at any time as many public washrooms do not supply anything on which to dry your hands.)

In general, make sure that you present a serious mature image. Japan is not the place to assert your individual tastes—not at least if you are trying to sell yourself.

Bowing

Bowing is an important and frequently observed part of Japanese culture. While you, as a foreigner, will not be expected to initiate a bow you will want to return one, so a little background on bowing will probably be useful. As Diana Rowland notes in her book *Japanese Business Etiquette*:

> "The basic ingredient in a bow is humility. You elevate, or honor, the other person by humbling yourself. The lower you bow, the more you honor the other party. Probably one of the most versatile human gestures, a bow can be used to convey numerous sentiments. For example, a superior can instantly communicate that a discussion is over with a quick bow."

Japanese bow often—when greeting or meeting someone, when offering a present or expressing congratulations or sympathy, when making a request or an apology, when indicating agreement, or when signaling closure of an event or imminent departure. It is almost an automatic reflex action, which is why you can observe people bowing even while talking on the telephone! Rowland mentions a survey conducted by a Japanese magazine, which found that "a typical businessman may bow 200 to 300 times a day, while a department store escalator girl who greets approaching customers may bow 2,000 to 3,000 times a day."

The Right Way to Bow

Bows are usually performed while standing with arms loosely at one's sides or, for women, crossed slightly in front. Bows begin at the waist with the back and neck stiff. The head remains in a straight line with the back. The younger or lower status person bows first and most deeply and holds the bow the longest. Most often, bows are held for only a second or two at about a fifteen degree angle. To a superior, a Japanese may bow as low as thirty degrees and may hold the bow for about three seconds. The depth of the bow and the length of time it is held depends on the relative age and status of the two people involved. Bows are generally deliberate gestures rather than simple acts of bobbing up and down. People often bow more than once, particularly when saying goodbye.

Companies coach both their male and female employees on proper bowing etiquette. Japanese office ladies in particular, will be greeting large numbers of senior company officials and important customers and are strongly encouraged to bow correctly. One Japanese company training video for female employees had a whole section devoted to the importance of greeting superiors and customers politely when passing them in the corridor. A machine directed beams of light to indicate the exact angle at which an office lady should bow.

Bowing is so automatic that it can sometimes take non-Japanese aback. I [Carin] remember once when a group of my Japanese friends were leaving my parents' house after dinner. As we were gathered in the doorway saying goodbye, my father bent down to pick a piece of fluff off the carpet. When he stood up, he found to his surprise that one of my friends, Yoshi, was returning his "bow."

As a foreigner, it is important that you make an effort to return a bow. The exact angle is not critical. You might find that some form of bowing comes to you quite automatically simply as a response to the bowing around you. Also, if for some reason you wish to convey regret or an apology, a deep long bow will probably convey this message best.

Seating Arrangements

Understanding Japanese views on seating arrangements is important whether you host Japanese business people or are their guest. If you are hosting Japanese visitors, here are a few pointers:

- Generally, guests should be seated on the side of the table away from the door (facing the door), while hosts have their backs to the door.
- If the two parties are seated on opposite sides of a table, the highest ranked person (or a spokesperson) sits in the middle. No one usually sits at the end of the table.
- If there is a blackboard at one end of the room or the chairperson is seated at the end of the table, then the highest ranking person should sit closest to the blackboard or the chairperson.
- The highest ranking person always sits down first. (Guests have higher status than hosts.)
- When a taxi driver or a chauffeur is driving, the highest ranked Japanese should be the first to enter and the last to exit the car and should sit behind the driver. (When there are four passengers, the highest ranking Japanese might also sit in the middle of the back seat.)
- When a colleague or the owner of the car is driving, the highest ranked person sits in the front passenger seat.

While as a guest, you are guided by your hosts as to where to sit (for example, side of the table away from the door with the most senior person in the centre), you have to decide where to locate the other members of your team. (When you are hosting Japanese visitors, you will also have to decide where to seat the members of your team.) It is important to recognize that the seating arrangements you choose send messages to your Japanese counterpart—whether or not you intend them to. It would, therefore, be wise to send the messages you wish to convey. This is particularly important when there are women, especially senior

Knowing Your Place

The Japanese are generally quite particular about seating arrangements in formal situations. If you are a guest in a Japanese office, it is best to follow the seating directions of your Japanese host.

If you are hosting Japanese visitors, here are a few pointers (O = most senior person in each group):

1. Generally, guests should be seated on the side of the table away from the door.

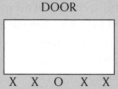

2. If the two parties are seated on opposite sides of the table, the highest ranked person sits in the middle.

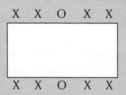

3. If there is a blackboard/whiteboard at one end of the room or a chairman at the end of the table, then the highest ranking people should sit closest to the board or chairman.

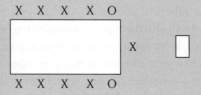

4. The highest ranking person should always sit down first.

5. In a taxi, the highest ranked person sits in the middle of the back seat.

6. If there are only two people in the back seat, the highest ranked person gets in first, followed by the lower ranked person.

7. When the owner is driving, the highest ranked person sits in the passenger seat.

women, on your negotiating team. In *Doing Business with Japanese Men: A Woman's Handbook*, Christalyn Brannen and Tracey Wilen share the results of interviews with over 200 women who do business with the Japanese. Many of these women mentioned the ways in which seating arrangements at initial meetings worked to establish or undermine their authority. Two examples underline this point:

Example 1
When I held my first meeting with the Japanese, I knew I had to establish my credibility immediately. I asked my team members to enter the room first, introduce themselves, and be seated. I told them not to start the meeting until I joined them and to leave the center seat at the negotiating table open for me. Better than any verbal introduction or business card, these very visible actions clearly established my position and authority. Equally important, they showed the Japanese that our negotiating team was unified and organized.

Example 2
As the last one to go into the meeting room I seated myself in the chair nearest the door. During the meeting, one of my male colleagues asked me to go photocopy a document since (he said later) I was in a convenient location. I did it, but it was hard for me to recover my credibility with the Japanese team. It looked like I was his secretary or his assistant, when in fact I was neither.

The bottom line then is to determine the signals you want to send, and plan the strategy and the seating of your team accordingly. A successful example follows:

Tom, my male colleague, and I have a female manager, Jane. We three realized that Tom, despite introductions to the contrary, might be perceived by the Japanese as the decision maker on our team. To avoid this possibility, we came up with the following plan. Jane, our manager, would make the introductory speech at the meeting, take the listener seat, and observe the meetings. I would take the center seat and be the speaker and analyzer of the negotiations. I would defer to Jane for important decisions and motion for her approval on agreements as they came up. During the meeting, Tom would sit by the door, make copies of all documents, assist the caterer, and take phone messages—as well as present his own part of the package. So although Tom would look after all the administrative duties, he would also be a key player. The final decisions, however, would always be made by Jane.

By positioning ourselves in this way we made the most of each of our roles. Sometimes a little finessing is necessary to establish the working relationship with the Japanese. We found that a little less rigidity in our roles was possible after the third or fourth meeting.

— *Doing Business with Japanese Men*, pp 36–37

More Than Meets the Eye

We have already discussed many of the elements of meeting etiquette, from seating arrangements to the handling of business cards. There is yet another aspect to keep in mind. In many meetings, senior executives might close their eyes during discussions and presentations. They are not, in most instances, asleep, and they are also not being rude. Rather, many Japanese business people find it easier to follow the flow of discussions if they keep their eyes closed. Do not assume that you have lost your audience. The closed eyes may well indicate that you have their full attention!

Gift Giving

Gift giving in Japan is an art (not to mention a $100 billion industry!) and is of the utmost importance as it centers around the concept of social reciprocity. The giving and receiving of gifts maintain and strengthen relationships. As Christopher Engholm notes, "Relationships are based on trust, dependency and obligation but reciprocity is their lifeblood." (Engholm p 68) Japanese know the debts owed by them and by others to them. Relationships are always in a dynamic state, each person always owing or being owed. One of the main ways for Japanese to maintain both their business and personal relationships, therefore, is through the exchange of gifts and favors. After receiving a gift, most Japanese will give a present in return. These kind of return gifts are called *o-kaeshi*. As Professor Helmut Morsbach, formerly of International Christian University in Tokyo notes, "Gift exchange is thus a serious matter because, once started, it is likely to continue into the indefinite future." Gifts are a method of keeping relationships functioning smoothly, of reaffirming one's commitment to the relationship. Professor Morsbach sums it up succinctly, "the function of gifts in Japan is much clearer than in the West: every one bears the invisible message "Forget me not!"

There are many words in Japanese to describe various kinds of gifts and gift giving, an indication of the prominence of gift giving in Japanese life. Professor Harumi Befu of Stanford University conducted a study in which he asked about 75 housewives to record all the gifts they had given and received over a seven-month period. Approximately 12,000 exchanges were recorded, with each household receiving about 13 gifts a month and giving about ten. These gifts ranged from small items such as hand towels from banks or service stations to fancy wedding presents. (As far as weddings are concerned, the most common gift is crisp new 10,000 yen notes placed in a decorative envelope. The amount varies depending on the person's relationship with the bride and groom. In return, at the reception, wedding guests receive an immediate return gift of some sort. Money is also given at funerals and again should be placed in the right kind of envelope. Ask for assistance in selecting the appropriate envelope in each case. These envelopes can be purchased from any convenience store (Source: Helmut Morsbach, "The Ritual of Japanese Gift Exchange," in *Winds* December 1987).

What is the Right Time for Gifts?

There are two primary gift giving periods. They are at the end of December (*oseibo*) and in mid summer (*ochugen*). Gifts are given to friends, colleagues, teachers, superiors, and clients; basically to anyone to whom one feels indebted in some way. According to one estimate, Japanese spend about $20 billion annually at oseibo! Popular presents include imported wine, high quality fruit (e.g. melons), tea or coffee sets, soap packages, dried goods, scotch whiskey, beer, condiments, rice crackers, sweets, or towel sets. Department stores often have gift counters where employees offer advice on the appropriate present. The ideal gift in this case is not a personal one so much as it is one that represents a certain monetary value. For this reason, many Japanese gift catalogues list their products by price range so that it is easy to find the value of product required. This can sometimes lead to people receiving many duplicate gifts as everyone gives the same "in" gifts. At different times, the "in" gifts have been salad oil, whiskey, and even toilet paper!

Gifts are also given at other times, such as when someone leaves on a long trip or when visiting Japanese at home. They are presented to offer sympathy or congratulations, or to express appreciation of past or anticipated kindness. When Japanese travel, whether within Japan or abroad, they are expected to bring presents for those people they are visiting and for those they have left at home. The thinking is that by being away, you have inconvenienced those left at home by making them do extra work to make up for your absence.

What are Good Gifts?

A Japanese business person will always bring a gift when visiting a company. The gift is intended as a sign of goodwill, not as a bribe. If you are doing business with a Japanese company, you should be prepared to exchange gifts. So, what kind of gift should you give in a business setting? If you are visiting Japan, it would be a good idea to bring presents from your home country. Duty-free stores or shops that cater to Japanese tourists would be good places to find suitable gifts. Specialty crafts or foods (wine, chocolates, expensive candy, smoked meats, or salmon); wall calendars or coffee table books with pictures of your home region; famous brand name items (Gucci, Louis Vuitton, Tiffany, or Christian Dior); or items from well-known stores (Harrods, Saks, or Marks and Spencer) make good gifts. As what is most important in Japanese gift giving is the giver's relationship with the recipient, personal gifts aside, the type of gift to give depends on the relative status of the two individuals and on the occasion. You might, therefore, also want to also have a number of small gifts for other more junior people you will be meeting. Pens, scarves, handkerchiefs, key rings, caps, T-shirts, golf balls, notebooks, and pins (any of these items could have the company logo on them) would all come in handy.

For those based in Japan, a Japanese colleague or friend might be able to give you advice on the gift to give depending on the circumstances. In the same way, as oseibo and ochugen gifts are often household products, so too are business gifts. It is crucial, though, to only give those goods in fancy gift packages. Most business gifts are bought at high-end department stores and wrapped in that store's paper to indicate the price and quality.

Dos and Don'ts of Gift Giving

- Gifts should be given and received with two hands as an indication of respect. Gifts are usually given while standing.
- Gifts are usually presented humbly, often with comments about the item being "nothing interesting" or of "little value."
- Gifts should be nicely wrapped. This is very important. Department stores will wrap items purchased from their store. Wrapping from a prestigious department store adds status to a present. Good colours for wrapping are brown, maroon, blue, purple, grey, and green. Avoid black and white, silver and white,

and yellow and white because they are associated with funerals. Red and white are wedding colours. If you are bringing a gift to Japan, you can sometimes have your hotel wrap it for you for a small charge.

- Gifts are not usually opened in front of the giver. If your hosts encourage you to open your present, by all means do so. Do not be surprised, however, if a gift you have given is simply set aside and opened after you have left.

- Avoid giving gifts in quantities of four or nine because of their association with death or suffering respectively.

- Avoid giving anything to do with cutting (i.e. knives or scissors) as those items are associated with the idea of severing the relationship.

- Make sure you thank the gift giver not only when you receive the gift but also the next time you speak or write to him or her. This should also be the case for any favours or kindness received.

- Whenever you give money, it should always be enclosed in paper or placed in an envelope.

- For a first meeting, some kind of corporate or group present is probably best. Some kind of sculpture or paperweight or photograph might be suitable. Present this toward the end of the meeting to the most senior person. If there is no appropriate time to give the gift, you can give it to a third party or go-between before or after the meeting, saying that it is a gift for the group and asking him or her to take care of it for you.

- Appropriate gifts for large groups are boxes of candies, cakes, or cookies (which can be easily shared around the office) or key rings, T-shirts, and caps. If you are giving individual gifts, make sure you have enough for all the people present. If you don't, give those gifts to your contact and have them distributed for you.

- Gifts to take to someone's home could include a gourmet food basket, wine, rice crackers, chocolates, or candies. Flowers are usually associated with romance or illness, so avoid giving them.

Entertaining Japanese in Your Home Country or in Japan

Entertaining is an important part of the business relationship with your Japanese counterparts whether you are in Japan or at home. Dining is an opportunity to get to know your business partners and to dissolve any tensions that might have arisen during the working day. Generally, business discussions are kept to a minimum. It is worthwhile knowing basic entertaining etiquette to be a good host to your Japanese visitors.

General Guidelines

Firstly, while in Western cultures it is often seen as most polite to give guests as many choices as possible, making these choices for the guest is the more polite course of action in Japan. At formal dinners, the entire menu will be planned ahead of time, and guests will not even see a menu. This is also the recommended way of proceeding when hosting Japanese visitors.

When dining at restaurants, it is preferable for the Japanese visitor to have the meal decided for him or her then to face the difficulty of reading the menu (the language in expensive restaurant menus tends to be fancy and difficult for the non-native English speaker to decipher) and then be bewildered by a myriad of choices from the waiter (from drinks to salad dressing to choice of vegetables). While it can be difficult to determine the best set meal to choose, it is worth the extra effort as your visitors will, no doubt, be more comfortable. Possible set menus could include steak, lamb, seafood, or a particular regional speciality. For a less formal meal (the second or third evening), a Chinese meal and a good Chinese restaurant would also be popular.

If for some reason, you cannot set the meal ahead of time, determine a few dinner choices you can recommend to your dining companions. Many Japanese, for example, like to try the regional or house speciality. Your visitors will most likely ask for your recommendation and follow it. Prepare your guests for the questions the waiter will ask them.

Be quite formal at the dinner. Give a welcoming speech, and propose a toast. Do not plan on having business discussions over dinner. Be prepared to talk about your region, the weather, Japan and Japanese culture, sports, company backgrounds, sports, and hobbies. Be prepared to pay for everything, and do so as discretely as possible, preferably away from the table. Many Japanese smoke so find out ahead of time whether smoking is permitted in the restaurant at which you will be dining. If not, advise your visitors ahead of time so they do not feel embarrassed.

While you will want to treat your Japanese visitors to a meal that is different from that to which they are accustomed, they are likely to crave some Japanese food after a few days. Providing them with a list of Japanese restaurants in the area, coupled with a map that shows how to get to those places, would be a nice touch. After the meal, escort your guests right to their hotel or taxi. Wait for the taxi with your guests until they get into it, and the cab is out of sight.

Along with dining out, other suitable kinds of entertainment would be local sightseeing tours, particularly to scenic sites, baseball games (most Japanese are big baseball fans), golf courses, shopping, or any special regional entertainment.

It is important that foreign business people take seriously the cultural and social elements of Japanese business rituals. These rituals are not quaint affectations of an ancient culture. They are vibrant, commonplace manifestations of contemporary Japanese values and expectations. To show a lack of respect for these rituals is to demonstrate a lack of respect for Japan. Local business people spend a lot of time to get the procedures and customs right, and they greatly appreciate the efforts of outsiders who conform to these same patterns. At the same time, business behavior that runs counter to Japanese expectations can be extremely counterproductive and can well result in difficulties in the commercial relationship.

This discussion on business rituals gives good examples of having cultural knowledge available within (or available to) your firm when dealing with the Japanese. Do not simply focus on the need to avoid making mistakes. Of more importance is your ability to provide your Japanese counterparts with a positive, culturally sensitive business environment. Once you do this, your personal and corporate standing will improve significantly.

CHAPTER 7

Japanese Business Culture

The rituals of business discussed early are the public manifestations of a complex and multilayered Japanese business culture. It is important to look beneath the surface and to assess both the substance of Japanese culture and to devise techniques for bringing cultural awareness into corporate operations. Japanese business people take cultural considerations very seriously, and expect the same in return. It is, thus, useful to consider some of the major cultural attributes of the Japanese and to discuss the steps that can be taken to ensure that your firm is well-situated for coping with these concerns.

Mount Fuji is perhaps the most famous location in Japan and attracts tens of thousands of visitors each year.

Harmony

Maintaining harmony, or avoiding open conflict, is one of the prime imperatives of Japanese business practice. While the Japanese are notoriously tough bargainers and are extremely persistent about the details of highly technical arrangements, they will also go to considerable lengths to avoid arguments, disagreements, and disharmony. The Japanese will, once they have established a partnership, be extremely anxious to please their counterpart—and will expect the same in return. They treasure their public reputation, but will openly apologize if they feel that their company or employees have somehow harmed a business relationship. The goal throughout is to maintain harmony and to minimize open conflict.

The pursuit of harmony takes precedence over almost all aspects of business life. It is not uncommon to suppress or control negative information if leading executives feel the news would disrupt the workforce. In business meetings, Japanese business people will express their *tatamae* feelings—opinions suitable for public consumption. Privately and away from the business setting, they might well express their *honne*, or true feelings. The willing suppression of negative viewpoints, bad news, or contradictory viewpoints is designed to protect a facade of harmony and collective understanding. If there are disagreements—as there invariably will be—they will generally be dealt with behind closed doors and even through third party arbitration.

The desire to create and ensure harmony also results in very strong pressure for consensus. (Note, again, the powerful influence of the group and the recurring requirement that individual expression and desires be subordinated to the wishes of the larger group.) Japanese decision making can take a very long time for precisely this reason. Face-to-face meetings with Japanese partners will be polite and pleasant, and the Japanese side will present a single impression and position. Outside the meeting and away from prying Western eyes, a lengthy process of consensus formation will occur, drawing recalcitrant employees into the circle. An employee in a Japanese organization seeking to push a particular objective will generally spend many hours in private consultations, gaining consensus before the item even reaches the floor for formal discussion. In this way, objections are heard privately, and open disagreement is avoided.

You can assist your Japanese counterparts in preserving harmony by following some very basic rules:

- Avoid open conflict, either within your group or between yourselves and your Japanese partners. Any such conflict will cause a deep rift and will make further discussions difficult.
- Do not expect a quick answer from Japanese partners. There is a consensus-building process that must occur—outside of your purview.
- Provide your Japanese contacts with as much advance information as you feel is necessary. Affording your potential partners an opportunity to discuss your concerns and proposals ahead of time may give them time to formulate a collective decision.
- Do not press for a decision. If the Japanese firm is taking its time, it generally means that there is significant opposition and that proponents are endeavouring to build additional support for the idea or the project. It is particularly inappropriate to try to circumvent the process by going to a senior executive in the hope that this individual will make a quicker decision. Such an intervention would cause a major "loss of face" and would likely earn the enmity of those avoided.

Building a Commercial Relationship

The greatest test of your adaptability to Japan will come when the negotiations commence. The Japanese are famous for their skills at negotiation and have a strong reputation for pushing very hard to get the best possible deals. It is always important to remember that the Japanese likely know far more about you—and Western customs and expectations generally—that you will know about them. And they will use this knowledge to their advantage. They will, at times, play on Western misunderstanding of Japanese culture, and otherwise will find ways to gain a commercial advantage. Within this context, it is possible to make some major errors that could easily upset otherwise mutually beneficial negotiations. Here are some general guidelines for negotiating with the Japanese:

- Approach negotiations with an understanding of Japanese business values.
- Recognize the importance of reciprocal obligations. Remember to return favors and invitations.
- Cultivate a long-term relationship. Do not rush a business negotiation in order to secure a short-term opportunity. The Japanese firm will, in all likelihood, be sizing your company up as a potential long-term partner. Once contacts have been made, cultivate the professional friendship and maintain the corporate relationship.
- The Japanese hold certain stereotypes about hard-driving, confrontational Westerners. Make sure that you do not conform to their expectations. The soft sell works much better.
- Don't be afraid to cut your losses. You are attempting to establish a long-term relationship. If it is obvious that an agreement cannot be reached, suggest a break or another meeting time.
- Show the Japanese that you are serious about developing a commercial arrangement. Send between two and four people as a negotiating team and include one senior executive. Continue to send the same team over the course of the negotiations as a way of building a personal relationship.
- Be prepared! Do your homework and come with the appropriate information and questions. Rest assured that the Japanese will be prepared for your visit. Research is essential, particularly if you

are working in a high-technology area. If your company is planning on licensing technology the Japanese require, make a thorough investigation of the research the Japanese company has been doing in your product area. (Use an on-site consultant.)

- Be alert for the "Yes that means No." The Japanese do not like to say "No" directly and, in fact, will go to great lengths to avoid doing so. Although there is a word for "No" in Japanese, most often the softer word *chigaimasu* ("it is different") is used. Saying "No" directly could offend someone or cause a conflict that would be better avoided. You should be able to pick up the clues that the answer is going to be "No." Watch for phrases like "That would be very difficult." You are being told, very politely, that what you want is unlikely.

- Watch for the "Yes that does not mean Yes." Foreigners often get confused because the Japanese will respond *Hait* ("Yes" or "I understand"), and will often say it quite strongly. They may not be actually saying "Yes." More likely, the comments means "I hear you". If you listen carefully, you can avoid the annoying experience of walking away from a meeting thinking that the issue has been settled when the Japanese believe that it remains unresolved.

- Enjoy the silences. Be prepared for long periods of silence in Japanese business meetings. Do not feel that you have to fill them in—a rather common Western practice. Silence does not mean that it is your turn to make a concession.

- Proceed on multiple fronts. In a standard Japanese business meeting, a variety of issues can be discussed simultaneously. No agreement is finalized on any of the items until the very end of the negotiations.

- Pay attention to the four stages of the business negotiation process. These stages will likely occur over several meetings. The Japanese prefer to proceed slowly and are often unimpressed with business people who push for a hasty resolution. North Americans tend to go quickly through the first two stages and concentrate on the third, while Japanese tend to emphasize stages one and two. Japanese negotiators tend to approach negotiations with an open mind to determine the possibilities.

1. **Pre-business**: The "getting to know each other" stage. Expect polite conversation.
2. **Information stage**: Both parties are attempting to find out each other's needs, preferences and the potential of the arrangement.
3. **Persuasion**: Each side is expected to present their case and try to win over the other side.
4. **Final Concessions and Agreement Stage**: Negotiations are concluded, bargaining is completed, and final compromises are struck.

- Do not enter negotiations with a fixed time of departure. You want to be in a situation to alter your plans to capitalize on the opportunity to close a business deal—or to be able to stick around to avoid a collapse of discussions.
- While the Japanese will go over business arrangements in exceptional detail, devoting a tremendous amount of time to relatively minor points, they tend not spend a lot of time bargaining on price. The first price on the table is usually close to what the Japanese want to pay. Take your guide as to the likely profitability of the discussions from this initial offer.
- Much the same goes for the specific details or language of a contract. Japanese dislike haggling over a contract because they do not attach much substantive importance to it. As one observer wrote, a contract is "more like a marriage document than a business agreement." (Zimmerman p 100) If they trust their partner, they will sign anything but they may wish to make changes later. A Japanese partner can feel almost betrayed if a foreign company insists on the fine print in a contract or is not willing to be flexible.

Culture Aspects of Marketing to the Japanese

Japan, despite its small size, is a maze-like consumer market—and great care must be taken to place products where consumers expect to find them and to ensure that potential customers learn about what you have to sell. It is extremely easy to get lost in the clutter of Japanese commerce. Annual consumer trade shows alone often attract hundreds of presenters, many of whom offer high-profile entertainment, glittery booths, and giveaways to gain attention. The country's media is similarly quite diverse (made more so recently by the expansion of satellite television). The Japanese are voracious consumers of newspapers and magazines—if only to keep themselves occupied on the daily commute. These, together with the ubiquitous train and billboard advertisements, are the primary means of reaching Japanese consumers.

Japanese advertising—and this should be no surprise by now—is quite unlike that in most other industrialized nations. Hard-hitting competitive advertisements are frowned upon. As Mitchel Deutsch once observed about advertising on television:

> "Television commercials should appear to the emotional and affective side of human nature, not the logical or scientific. The Japanese distrust experts and consultants, so overloading an advertising theme with advice, statistics, and scientific studies does not generally sway the Japanese. The soft sell is the preferred, and usually it is the only sell. Ads should aim for a gut reaction with repetitive themes or jingles that let viewers know intuitively that a certain product is 'right' and will enhance their positions in their communities."
>
> — *Doing Business with the Japanese,* p 165

To criticize a competitor publicly is considered bad form. Instead, Japanese advertisements tend to work on creating a specific mood and ambiance—and the better ads speak directly to Japanese assumptions and values. Japanese firms often use Western entertainers and sports stars in their advertisements—typically performing roles that they would never accept in North American or Europe. (This, in turn, explains why these same personalities generally require that their "unique" Japanese advertisements not be shown outside the country.) Importantly, offering discounts is not often an effective strategy when introducing a product into Japan; linking the item to a low price will tend to "cheapen" the product image and discourage purchasers.

Product placement is also key—and requires greater attention than in countries with large networks of department stores. It is important to meet Japanese consumers where they are—and that is typically on the move. While there has been a slight move toward the construction of large department stores, this is typically restricted to a few communities around Tokyo. The nation is really one of small shops and specialty stores. Within Tokyo, there are whole regions that specialize in select products. Akihabara, for example, offers one of the most concentrated offerings of electronic goods in the world. The Ginza district is world-famous for its high-class entertainment. There are specific areas in the city for restaurant supplies, cultural materials, and others. A vast network of tiny convenience stores, matched with equally small and highly specialized restaurants, make up a huge portion of the country's businesses. And the movement of millions of Japanese commuters through train and subway stations means that the shopping corridors in these areas offer a prime means of reaching consumers.

These are not the only avenues available for businesses seeking to gain the attention of Japanese consumers. The Japanese are inveterate catalogue shoppers and make numerous purchases each year from the thousands of catalogues available in the country. This provides a prime opportunity for foreign companies who wish to test the Japanese market without making large initial investments in physical facilities. The Internet provides yet another opportunity. After an early reluctance to capitalize on the commercial potential of the Internet to sell to the Japanese, foreign corporations have been racing to set up Japanese-language web sites and to provide services to Japanese customers. National firms, in contrast, have moved much more cautiously into this small but growing market. Similarly, international firms have capitalized on the attractiveness of door-to-door or direct marketing—yet another way of meeting the needs of consumers who have little time for shopping.

Marketing to the Japanese requires careful attention to cultural details. An American firm once marketed tennis balls in lots of four—the number that signifies death in Japan. Not a big seller! On a different level, packaging assumes a significance in Japan that has more to do with aesthetics than commerce. Japanese stores and supermarkets wrap their products exquisitely, and consumers expect that level of attention to detail and presentation. For the same reason, economy packs are generally used only for mundane items or those sold to institutions. Clearly, the warehouse approach now commonplace in many Western countries will find few (some, but not many) followers in Japan. Marketing, more than any other part of the business enterprise, has to be handled in a culturally-sensitive fashion. This is particularly the case in Japan.

Women and Business in Japan

We have incorporated comments on the specific experiences of business women throughout the text. Japanese businessmen have, over the past decade, become aware that, in the global marketplace, they are likely to be dealing with foreign business women from time to time. While there are many stories from previous decades where foreign business women were dealt with dismissively, the situation has improved considerably.

The situation for women in Japan has been changing in recent years. Japanese women are, themselves, becoming more prominent in business and it is becoming increasingly common to encounter women at senior executive levels. Long-standing assumptions about young women who would work only until they married and generally in very basic positions are being challenged. Women still encounter considerable workplace discrimination and examples of sexist behavior abound (as they do in many cultures!), but an increasing number of Japan women are opting for full professional careers and are emerging in leadership roles within their companies. Foreign businesswomen are likely to want to absent themselves from some aspects of after-hours socializing; their absence, while noted, will not generally be held against them.

Role of Cultural Advisors and Interpreters

You will, over time, come to appreciate the subtle nuances of Japanese business culture. In the first instance, however, you may find the assumptions that underlie Japanese commerce to be more than a little baffling. It is important that you not simply "wing it" in Japanese business. Find a trained cultural advisor and/or interpreter to assist with your initial business contacts and meetings. And once you have selected an advisor/interpreter, pay attention to what they tell you to do. If they suggest that you sit in a certain place, do so. If they recommend that you not use a particular phrase, slogan or approach, consider yourself well-advised.

The cultural complexity that we have described earlier in the book has a variety of implications for the foreign business operating in Japan. As described, marketing operations, staff recruitment, product selection and placement, and dozens of other aspects of commercial activities will be strongly influenced by cultural and social considerations. Hiring a suitable advisor is essential if you hope to avoid some of the major errors that have accompanied earlier attempts to enter the Japanese market. Remember, particularly if the advisor you have selected is a Japanese person, that they are likely to be very anxious to please and very reluctant to speak to you sharply or harshly. Pay attention to subtle comments and suggestions; in Japanese terms, a very subtle rebuke can be the equivalent of being yelled at in Western circles.

Interpreters are essential for companies that do not have skilled Japanese speakers on staff. You will leave yourself at a significant disadvantage if you do not have the capacity to understand the conversation at a meeting. Both sides should bring an interpreter to a business meeting. Do not rely on the interpreter of your counterparts, and do not expect your opposite numbers to use your advisor. Often members of the Japanese team will speak English but they still bring an interpreter for extra clarification and to give themselves extra time to digest and consider information. Pretending not to understand your counterparts' language can also be a useful way to hear what they are saying among themselves. Interpreters also supply cultural information that can be invaluable. Relying on the other negotiating team's interpreter puts your group at a disadvantage.

Your interpreter acts as a transmitter, not just of your words and ideas but often of your humor, intelligence, and personality. A good interpreter will convey as much of the emotion of the speaker as possible. Make sure then that when you respond to that which is being interpreted, you respond to the speaker and not to the interpreter. Here are some general tips for making effective use of an interpreter:

- Find a good interpreter. You can find specialists in particular fields of business, so look out for the kind of interpreter you need. Japanese interpreters can be very expensive, but do not try to save money by hiring someone without the proper credentials or experience.
- Brief the interpreter. Give him/her as much information ahead of time as possible. Meet with the interpreter and explain the kind of meeting and the vocabulary needed. Describe as much of the business situation as you can, and tell the interpreter what you hope to get out of the meeting. If someone is going to give a speech, give it to the interpreter ahead of time.
- Limit your sentences to a maximum of 7 to 15 words. Shorter sentences make it easier for your audience to follow your train of

thought. They are also more manageable for the interpreter to remember and interpret.

- Speak for short periods. Two or three sentences at a time would be a good guideline to follow.
- Do not interrupt the interpreter. Allow sufficient time for him/her to keep up with the speaker. Due to the need for honorific (polite language) and indirect expression, it takes 30% longer to say things in Japanese than in English, so do not be surprised by the delays or extra words in the interpreter's translation of your comments.
- Do not be surprised if the interpreter consults a dictionary. No one can know all the technical words in two languages.
- Eliminate your use of idiomatic expressions or slang. These do not translate well.
- Look at the person to whom you are speaking and not at the interpreter.
- Have your interpreter debrief you after the meeting. There are many things that the interpreter may have heard or observed that would be useful for you to know.

Japanese business culture is an extension of the society in which it sits. It is relatively easy to figure out the business conventions and rituals that govern commercial relations. It takes far longer to understand the underlying values and attitudes. The temptation—because aspects of Japanese culture are different—is to make light of the differences and to see them as inconsequential. Quite the opposite is the truth. The Japanese are very proud of their culture and of what they see to be their national distinctiveness. Outsiders often see the belief in such things as harmony to be a quaint "Asian affectation," but they are central to Japanese thought and action.

Long-term success in Japanese business rests in understanding the cultural complexities that influence the business environment.

Once these cultural realities are understood and meshed into corporate operations, the firm will have a strong chance of profiting in Japan. If the company, in contrast, attempts to stay aloof from these Japanese realities and endeavors to operate as though Western values are dominant or more appropriate, employees can expect to encourage considerable resistance and an endless series of small, little-spoken difficulties with Japanese consumers and partners. Learning to think like the Japanese and to incorporate Japanese values into company business practices, is an essential element in adapting to Japan

CHAPTER 8

A Strategy for Business Success in Japan

International business textbooks are full of stories about foreign companies that had failed in their attempts to break into the potentially lucrative Japanese market. In case after case, companies are pilloried for misreading Japanese culture, sympathized with for running into the brick wall of Japanese bureaucracy, chided for failing to adapt their products to suit local consumer tastes, or criticized for not taking time to research the intricacies of the Japanese business environment. The cumulative message is very simple: doing business in Japan is tough, Japanese cultural nationalism interferes with attempts by foreign corporations to the enter the domestic market, and great caution must be exercised before venturing into the uncertain waters of Japanese business. The message is clear, but is it fair?

The "horror" stories of old have a little grain of truth, caused by a mixture of Western arrogance and Japanese recalcitrance. Many foreign business people have, historically, approached Japan with the idea that Japanese assumptions, social rituals, and business practices are irrelevant if not laughable. More than once, open expressions of foreign arrogance have killed potentially promising business deals. Even more routinely, outsiders do not realize how their insensitivity to the nuances of local practices has scuttled an otherwise promising opportunity. There is, to put it delicately, a residue of cultural superiority and self-centeredness attached to most North American, Australasian, and European businesses (and, in other cases, including many Asian business people, more than a little lingering historical animosity toward the Japanese).

Business people approaching Japan have to recognize that the Japanese, like all other people in the world, like to be taken seriously, expect to have their cultural norms respected, and bristle at any sign of anti-Japanese sentiment or foreign "arrogance." And the Japanese market, to be clear, has been difficult, historically unwelcoming, and tied up in a fancy menage of government red tape and the intricacies of the Japanese commercial marketplace.

Since the re-evaluation of the yen as part of the Plaza Accord of 1985, however, the Japanese commercial market has changed dramatically. The Japanese government has, through JETRO, invested billions of yen in a concerted effort to encourage importers.

Japanese consumers' interest in foreign trade goods remains strong, although still tempered by the niceties of local taste and custom. More importantly, Japanese businesses are focusing first and foremost on the domestic market, testing out new products and services locally before exporting them overseas. Even the recent financial crisis contains seeds of opportunities. In the aftermath of a series of bank and investment company failures, the Japanese government has taken steps to open up financial and insurance markets to outside firms. Add to this the increased global interest in free trade and continued international pressure on Japan to liberalize trading regulations and you have a situation well-suited for foreign businesses to thrive in Japan.

Whatever the situation in the past, the contemporary business environment is relatively favorable and the large, innovative, and constantly evolving Japanese consumer and industrial markets hold enormous potential for firms willing to take the time and effort necessary to establish a presence in the country. But it is imperative that potential investors or traders recognize the fundamental importance of cultural sensitivity and of understanding the nuances of Japanese society. Far too many excellent business deals have collapsed due to cultural misunderstanding. Many foreign businesses have missed opportunities to expand due to their failure to recognize commercial openings or to make the necessary first small steps toward solidifying a commercial relationship. (A recent visit to a frequent flyer lounge at Narita International Airport provided a sad lesson on how little things had changed. Several business people, making no effort to keep their ideas to themselves, offered gratuitous and sharply negative assessments of Japanese culture and society. Old stereotypes do, indeed, die hard.)

Unless business people are prepared to approach Japan on its terms and to work within the country's commercial structures, doing business in Japan can be a long, expensive, and unhappy process. Foreigners must recognize the strengths and weaknesses of the contemporary economic order and be prepared to look beyond the time-honored stereotypes of the geisha, sumo wrestler, and samurai. They would then have taken the first step toward commercial success in the Japanese marketplace.

Contacts and More Contacts

Japan works on a finely tuned network of personal and professional contacts. At times, as with the recent spate of financial scandals involving government employees and leading companies, these connections become a little too cozy. But contacts and introductions are essential for commercial success. While it takes time to build up connections, the effort is generally well worthwhile. Japanese business people prefer to deal with individuals that they know and trust.

Once a relationship is established, it becomes an integral part of corporate operations and can help businesses maintain contact through difficult times. Within Japanese businesses, these contacts are generally made through school and, particularly, university. Personal friendships often mature into long-lasting and mutually beneficial commercial relationships. As one endeavors to work through the often baffling maze of government regulations and commercial relations, it helps immensely if a company's efforts are backed up by a web of contacts.

Building connections can be a time-consuming process. It requires a fair deal of entertaining—the oil that lubricates Japanese business—and a great deal of sincerity. Successful business dealings will likely result in offers to assist with further contacts. Harsh encounters in the business world almost certainly ensure that contacts will evaporate. (The logic here is quite fundamental: the person providing the contact is placing some of his/her credibility on the line when recommending a business person. Should the encounter prove unsatisfactory, the individual who made the initial recommendation is bound to face embarrassment.)

Most foreign business people develop their initial contacts through Japanese firms doing business in their country and through the Japanese embassy at home and their national embassy in Japan. Much more rides on the ability of these embassy officials to develop and maintain contacts than is generally appreciated; the fact that many are recruited away from the embassies to work for foreign business based in Japan is a prime indication of the success of many of these individuals. Membership in business and professional associations and social clubs can help, as can attendance at official functions.

The use and development of contacts in Japan is not an invitation toward corruption or backdoor dealing. Contacts and recommendations are personal, not financial. The goal is not to enrich individuals, but rather to provide assurances that people being recommended are reliable, trustworthy, and honorable. Gaining the confidence of government and company officials is, therefore, essential if the company is to succeed in Japan, for a strong network of contacts is evidence of considerable personal and corporate credibility. Once contacts are made, they should be carefully cultivated so as to ensure their continued viability. Maintaining regular communication, taking an interest in the personal and professional life of the contact, and making sure that the relationship is reciprocal is essential. Contacts are not one-way streets, and returning favors granted is an important part of the business process in Japan.

Taking the Long View—Persistence and Continuity in Commercial Relations

Japanese businesses plan for the very long term. In a country where it is possible to take out a 100-year mortgage, it is perhaps not surprising that corporate leaders are as concerned about the year 2020 as they are about 2000. (Some companies have one or two hundred year plans.) This does not mean that Japanese firms ignore short-term considerations and are oblivious to commercial basics. The opposite is closer to the truth, in that they can be distressingly precise and preoccupied with minute details of contracts, schedules, quality measures, and the like. At the same time, however, the Japanese realize their economic vulnerability and have sought ways to protect themselves from the vagaries of the ever-changing marketplace.

This long-term perspective shows up in a number of ways. Japanese manufacturers are very concerned about the supplies of raw materials. Leaving little to chance and having learned a painful lesson from the oil shocks of the 1970s, they have taken the lead in developing new mines. They have secured access to forest resources and built railways in underdeveloped areas of Asia to get required materials. Time and time again, Japanese firms have signed lengthy contracts or development deals to ensure that the company and the nation have a steady stream of the supplies necessary to keep the industrial sector going. Japanese companies also invest very heavily in research and development, and encourage all employees to contribute to product design and internal innovation. Government strategy is forward-looking, seeking to anticipate social trends and demographic transitions.

For foreign business people, perhaps the most important aspect of the Japanese long-term outlook is their reliance on personal and professional relationships. Japan is not yet a particularly litigious society. The Japanese look askance at the time and expense devoted to lawyers in the United States and other Western countries. There is a stronger sense of interrelationship and of lasting corporate partnerships explicit in the keiretsu, which permeates Japanese commercial culture. Japanese firms are rarely interested in short-term, one-off deals. They seek, instead, to develop a business relationship and are prepared to spend several years ensuring that the foundations for a long-term partnership are well and truly laid. This approach is deeply ingrained in the social formalities that surround Japanese business contacts (see chapter 6).

Japan is not a good place for those seeking quick profits and a fast turnaround. Negotiations on initial contracts can take a very long time. Japanese business people will generally be sizing up a potential business partner with a view to a lengthy, mutually beneficial relationship. They will be wary of anyone seeking to sign a quick deal and have had considerable experience with foreign firms who are not prepared to stick around over the long-haul. Suspicion of foreign motivations abounds in Japan. Local firms look for partners who care about the country, take time to learn its intricacies, and who share a concern about building long-term arrangements. There are many places in the world where a "get rich quick" approach to business can succeed. Japan is not one of them.

The recent financial crisis provides a good case in point. Many foreign firms have been scared off Japan by routine stories about the economic and political difficulties. Japanese companies, however, prize loyalty, and they will be particularly impressed by companies (and countries) that stand by them during these tough times. Equally, firms that venture into the Japanese market now, when many foreign companies are either delaying their plans or scaling back on their intended operations, will likely find that they have earned considerable goodwill. Japan's current economic morass is unlikely to continue for long. Kudos and improved commercial opportunities await those firms who stick with the Japanese economy through the tough years.

The basic point here is a simple one. Do not look to Japan for a quick turnaround. It will take months, even years, to establish a strong, on-going commercial relationship. While some short-term benefits are possible as potential partners feel each other out, the real profits and opportunities lie in the future. Foreign businesses hoping to succeed in Japan have to take matters slowly, amass cultural knowledge and contacts, develop personal and professional relationships, become comfortable with the Japanese way of doing business, and demonstrate an on-going commitment to the Japanese market. The rewards can be considerable, for the Japanese market remains rich, vital, and innovative. But do expect to go slow and to experience some frustrations. Persistence will pay off.

Finding the Right Staff

Hiring and training personnel is fundamental to the success of any business, but there are some special considerations to take into account when dealing with Japan. It is axiomatic in companies involved in international trade that prolonged periods of work overseas can actually inhibit career progression. As a result, Japan-based employees of foreign companies tend to stay a relatively short time, either returning to their home country or being recruited by another Japan-based international firm. Raiding of foreigners who are already based in Japan is increasing as companies endeavor to find individuals with language skills and cultural sensitivity. Individual companies, however, generally experience considerable turnover in their Japan-based personnel.

For many firms, the solution has been to hire Japanese nationals. Until recently, there was considerable risk involved in such a strategy. The country's commitment to lifelong employment meant that employees moving outside the Japanese corporate world faced the prospect of an uncertain future. As a consequence, finding suitable employees was often very difficult. The economic changes in the last decade, particularly sizable layoffs in middle and senior management, have released a cadre of Japanese nationals into the workforce and made it easier for foreign businesses to find individuals willing to work for them. Interviews with Japan-based foreign firms revealed that finding good management staff remained a formidable challenge. Foreign firms look for different things in a Japanese employee compared with a similar Japanese company. Hence, an individual who succeeds in a Japanese firm might not do that well in a foreign organization. Incoming firms are looking for individuals with considerable flexibility, the ability to innovate, an openness to new challenges, and new ways of doing business. This series of requirements is very different from the qualities sought by most Japanese companies.

Hiring Japanese nationals carries many benefits, not the least which are linguistic ability, cultural knowledge, and the network of contacts so essential to business success. Many foreign companies identify their Japanese employees as their most vital commercial assets and speak very highly of the contributions that they make to the firm. At the same time, recruiting Japanese managers can segregate the Japanese operations from domestic activities and limit the exchange of information within the company. It is worth noting that Japanese companies operating overseas are far more likely to have Japanese managers in senior positions. In most business fields, however, it would be extremely difficult to operate in Japan without a significant number of senior Japanese employees.

Many smaller firms, particularly those venturing into Japan for the first time, rely on short-term Japanese consultants and translators. The advantages of such a strategy are obvious: low cost, local knowledge, facility with the language, and potentially valuable contacts in the field. There are a large number of well-trained, well-connected consultants available to assist foreign companies in their initial forays into Japan. Such an arrangement, however, means that the firm's lead individual in Japan is a temporary employee who has little or no understanding of the corporate culture, product lines, or company objectives. While the consultants can be extremely helpful in the short term and can help avoid cultural misunderstandings in Japan, they generally provide little long-term continuity. Equally important, they play a minimal role in educating the head office and domestic employees of the intricacies of Japanese business.

Foreign firms have been remarkably slow in developing their domestic capacity in the area of Japanese business. Even companies that make millions of dollars of business annually with Japanese partners rarely employee full-time Japan specialists, preferring to rely on short-term, contract translators and advisors. Japanese businesses, in contrast, often have several employees with specialized knowledge of their partner country (gained through study or work experiences abroad). Larger Japanese firms employ sizable contingents of market analysts, who keep a watch on their international trading partners and who are ready to alert their employers to any significant developments. Foreign companies, on the other hand, tend to devote little time to such exercises. Consequently, they are often ill-informed about the nuances of political, economic, and social changes.

If your company is serious about Japan, it is important that the firm trains staff members in the Japanese language, as well as the necessary cultural and business knowledge. This can be by way of an ongoing relationship with a Japan-based consultant, with the caveats noted above. Conversely, the company could recruit a specialist in the field, send senior managers to work in Japan for significant stretches of time, or train junior employees to ensure that the firm has and maintains the necessary expertise. The easiest option, and one that is increasingly being adopted, is to hire a foreigner who already lives in Japan. (Here again, the pattern of loyalty to an employer provides an advantage, in that money spent training and developing staff tends to stay with the company. In many other countries, employee mobility can mean that the skills gained at considerable cost and effort can easily be lost to the firm.)

Given the complexity, cultural richness, innovation, and economic transitions in Japan, it is vital that the foreign firm wishing to trade in Japan be well educated about the country. It is equally important that this education become an integral part of operations and not an "as required" consultation with a contract professional.

Having the Right Product

Japanese consumers are among the most innovative, flexible, and creative in the world. This vast domestic market has managed to find room for some of the strangest commercial products imaginable, ranging from *tamagotchis* to dancing flowers. These same consumers generally have very high standards—they expect the product to work and to work well. And they tend to replace items quickly. The Japanese place a high priority on having "new" items at hand. (This, in turn, is a function of the small size of most Japanese homes. There is very little room to store items no longer in use.)

For many years, the Japanese consumer market was extremely imitative. While food and restaurant markets were strongly tipped in favor of traditional tastes and customs, clothing, electronics, and other goods were patterned on Western products. The Japanese government helped keep competitors at bay, imposing a series of baffling duties and restrictions designed to protect local industry. The difficulties involved in getting brand name Western products no doubt added to their allure.

The government has been reducing trade barriers in recent years, and the reorientation of the economy to meet domestic needs has sparked a veritable revolution in consumer products and retailing. Japanese stores are filled with an amazing variety of products—and the service sector is just as diverse—in their haste

Akibabara is the electronics district of Tokyo.

to satisfy consumer demands. These transitions, in turn, have created opportunities for foreign businesses, including those able to trade on the continued Japanese interest in brand names and premium quality products and their openness to new items. (Local fascination with electronics is perhaps the best example; the Tokyo district of Akihabara, or Electric City, is one of the world's primary centres for consumer electronics.) Companies with innovative products would do well to test the Japanese market.

This all said, Japanese consumers are very particular. They expect to have products adapted to local requirements (for example Japanese language packaging) and tastes (that is with an emphasis on compactness). Whether the product is a new computer peripheral or aluminum ingots, Japanese purchasers generally know what they want and will not settle for less. This preoccupation with specifics often irritates foreign business people, who are used to working in more "forgiving" consumer markets. The trick in Japan is to do careful market research and to ensure that the product on offer addresses local needs. An item that is price competitive and technologically superior might well languish on the shelves for want of attention to the subtleties of the Japanese market.

Quality and Dependability

As has already been suggested, perhaps the most important aspect of the Japan market is that the Japanese expect their foreign partners to operate according to Japanese principles. Since Japanese consumers have exceptionally high standards and are willing to pay a premium for high quality products, Japanese businesses likewise emphasize the need for quality. Because Japanese consumers have very high expectations from service personnel and expect prompt delivery and production, Japanese businesses expect similar standards from their suppliers and service providers. When Japanese businesses then kick up a fuss about the inability of a foreign partner to meet exacting standards or to deliver services or products as promised, they are only imposing the same standards that apply to themselves. Although it may not seem so at times, most foreign markets operate according to more lax standards and lower (or more realistic) expectations. Stories abound about contracts voided for failing to meet exacting deadlines and about non-Japanese firms driven to distractions by their Japanese partners' fanatical attention to detail.

Not surprisingly, this commitment to high quality has percolated through the Japanese economy. Consumers readily—even enthusiastically—pay premium prices for products that achieve the appropriate standard. Oftentimes, and this is where Japan differs significantly from other economies, there is a much smaller market for cheaper and lower quality products. (This may be changing as large superstores specializing in discount items set up shop on the outskirts of major cities.) Most foreign businesses seeking to enter the Japanese consumer market will be aiming for the high-end segment—and will therefore be expected to compete as much on quality as price with domestic producers and other foreign firms.

Strangely enough, the quality issue is the one element that generally trips up foreign businesses seeking to do business in Japan. Many firms find it difficult, even irritating, to be expected to produce to a different, more exacting standard for the Japanese market than for their domestic consumers. Images of the near-obsessiveness of Japanese middlemen (who know only too well the complaints and criticism that will come down the line) over the quality of incoming merchandise are legendary, accurate, and disturbing. Stories of profitable contracts lost due to a short-term drop in quality control make non-Japanese businesses very nervous about dealing in the Japanese market. In some countries, international executives readily understand the importance of high quality to the Japanese purchasers but have difficulty conveying the urgency of the matter to all in the company.

Quality pays—in the Japanese market more so than in most countries. A corporate commitment to achieving and maintaining high standards is an essential element of long-term trade relationships with Japan and can provide an excellent foundation for commercial success in the country. While the Japanese concern with quality may seem a little "over the top" at times, it is a core element in their business culture and hence must be heeded.

Understanding Japan's Challenges

In chapter 2, we described some of the challenges currently facing Japan. Some of these—the dynamics of population, the aging of Japanese society, and the high cost of housing—are formidable problems. But it is an old axiom of business that one person's difficulties are another's opportunities. This is particularly true in Japan. The country is experiencing considerable internal change and will continue to wrestle with these challenges in the years to come. Local intelligence should, therefore, be an integral part of any foreign businesses strategy for dealing with Japan (or any country, for that matter).

Take, for example, the reality of Japan's aging population. While the growing number of senior citizens is causing the Japanese government considerable difficulty, the upside is the potential of an enormous market. Many of these seniors have considerable wealth, unique needs, and a willingness to try new products and services. Companies that have the right products and are willing to adapt either the product, the marketing, or the delivery system to meet Japanese expectations might well find an impressive market opportunity in the midst of this social situation.

The recent financial crises provide a good case in point. Regular readers of the Western press would sense that Japan is mired in a serious economic downturn. Without downplaying the significance of current difficulties, some perspective is needed. By international standards, Japanese unemployment and inflation are low. Consumer purchases have shifted a little—less overseas travel (but not as much of a decline as is often suggested), and a greater emphasis on local entertainment, for example—but the country's retail sector remains reasonably strong.

In 1998, consumer spending and consumer confidence dropped and, the next year, the government distributed vouchers to parents and senior citizens. These vouchers are to be used on purchases (that is, they cannot be saved) in the hope that a rush to the market will improve the retailing picture. Products that fit into that broad niche between essential items and luxury goods might well prove attractive to the millions of consumers who will have access to these vouchers and who will be expected to use them quickly. Most countries around the world would consider Japan's economic fundamentals, save for a steady increase in government spending, to be quite acceptable. And most Japanese citizens have enjoyed a fairly reasonable standard of living over the past decade. While the financial troubles should send out a warning, Japan's domestic economy remains more vibrant and dynamic than the international press suggests.

A central element in a corporate strategy for success in Japan involves a concerted effort to keep abreast of the political, social, and cultural happenings in the country. One used to be able point to the absence of foreign language analysis as a reason for staying aloof from the intricacies of Japanese politics, administration, and cultural life. No longer. There a vast array of intelligent and informed commentary on Japan—the *Japan Times*, regular coverage in the *Economist*, the *Far East Economic Review*, and dozens of other timely and helpful publications. As well, it is important that analysts look not just at the short-term political and financial developments but also follow long-term social, economic, cultural, and political trends. There is a vast array of opportunities to be found in the country's efforts to address the needs of its aging population. The demand for services in rural Japan creates openings for companies involved in information technology, tele-health, and related fields.

Taking Japan Seriously

When outsiders first reached Japan, they were awed by the mystery of the place, the seeming impenetrability of Japanese society, and the nuances and obliqueness of local customs. In a centuries-long process of creating and defining the "orient," people of other cultures wrapped Japan in a shroud of mysticism. At times, this evolved into simplistic stereotypes: the barbaric militarism, Japanese backwardness, and the country's shameless imitation of the West. These images were hardened by World War II and remain in evidence across large parts of the world. The complexity of the Japanese language and the seeming aloofness of the country and its people only added to the misunderstanding.

Business people hoping to succeed in Japan should get to know and respect the place. It is always quite remarkable to find individuals who, although active in Japanese business for a decade or longer, have made no attempt to learn the local language or to develop more than a passing familiarity with local customs or culture. Japan is an intriguing place—learning about it carries its own rewards. At the same time, getting to know the country can produce significant commercial opportunities.

By moving past stereotypes and by beginning to understand the nuances of Japanese society, a well-educated business person can give himself/herself an enormous personal and professional edge. Remember—and this is a vital caveat—that the Japanese generally understand the non-Japanese world much better than foreign business people understand Japan. For decades, the advantage had rested with the Japanese, and they have repeatedly capitalized on and developed that leverage. Successful foreign business people in Japan do not recoil at the complexity of the country, nor do they surrender to the simplicity of widely held stereotypes. Instead, they seek to understand their future and potential business partners within their national and cultural context.

How Not to Do Business with the Japanese

Public appearances are very important to the Japanese. It is imperative for foreign business people to recognize that "losing face" in a business or professional setting is extremely painful for Japanese executives. Consider one story, recounted by Richard Lewis, in *When Cultures Collide*.

Lewis and his business partner were attempting to lease a building in Japan. They met with an aging company president who proceeded, at considerable length, to explain the merits of the building and to outline the rental charges. When the president finished, Lewis's partner quickly jumped in and offered him half the requested rental fee. The president stood up and left the room. The meeting was over, and no subsequent meetings were held. The problem was not the counter-offer—bargaining is part of business in Japan, as is anywhere in the world. Rather, the difficulty rested with behavior that the Japanese president would see as rude and aggressive. The potential reenters had not treated the president with sufficient respect.

How is this done? The first requirement—interest—is the easiest to provide but is often the most elusive. It is depressing to watching foreigners shy away from Japanese foods, avoid intensely Japanese settings, and seek out a non-Japanese cocoon. It is even more depressing to hear the callous, even unfriendly comments from some business people about their Japanese counterparts. And it is delightful, in the extreme, to speak to non-Japanese business people who have embraced Japan, in all of its strengths and weaknesses and who have learned to live and flourish within its boundaries. Once eyes have been opened to the nation's potential, the rest flows easily.

The numerous books on the country, many helpful and some misleading, provide useful insights. Experiencing the country, particularly by moving beyond Tokyo, offers striking and direct illustrations of the nature and character of the people and the land. Participating in cultural events and visiting major cultural shrines give the nation's history a sense of immediacy and potency. And nothing helps as much as making friends within the country, for their guidance and wisdom will quickly prove invaluable in navigating the shoals of Japanese customs and traditions.

It is important to realize that the Japanese, like all other people, do not expect perfection from outsiders and newcomers. What they do desire is respect and effort. Even the slightest effort at learning the language or remembering an important cultural attribute can bring the widest smile and the heartiest congratulations. A business person can make one major error in approaching Japan, and that is aloofness. Japan is a country to be enjoyed and to be immersed in. It is not a nation or a society that can be understood from the outside. Taking Japan seriously and getting to know the country and its people carry immense personal rewards and, to a greater degree than in most places, significant commercial and professional benefits as well.

Basic Facts and Travel Tips

Business people entering a new business environment typically do so with a mix of enthusiasm and concern. Beyond professional considerations—making contacts, conducting business meetings, negotiating contracts, and the like—lie a series of more practical matters, like eating, sleeping, traveling, and relaxing. Many foreign business people, particularly those from the West, are a little nervous about visiting Japan, knowing only too well the barriers of language and custom that stand before them. Worries about the basics, such as the availability of food and the necessity of eating Japanese-style cuisine, only adds to the anxiety.

What follows addresses some of the concerns. Remember that Japan is an extremely safe country, and foreigners generally encounter few hassles or dangerous situations. Also, the Japanese

The Japanese travel widely within their own country. Here, a family poses for a picture in front of the temple in Asakusa.

are very helpful. Standing in a public location, starring in puzzlement at a local map, is often sufficient to elicit several offers of assistance. The transit system seems chaotic; it is not. In fact, it is quite easy to figure out. The road and address system, in contrast, is extremely complicated—most businesses will provide faxed maps of the best route to their office from the nearby train and subway stations—and finding your way around individual neighborhoods can be very difficult.

Japanese food is remarkable in its diversity and quality—and the ubiquitous fast-food restaurants ensure a ready supply of inexpensive, familiar Western-style food.

Japan is a unique country, and many aspects of the social and cultural order will appear a little unusual at first. But do take time to explore its rich diversity, whether you do this solely within a major city (getting to know Tokyo would take more than a lifetime) or by traveling around the country. Sample the country's rich cultural entertainment. There should be a prize for staying awake during *Noh* theatre, but *Kabuki* plays are delightful. Japanese sporting events, particularly professional baseball, are enough to re-establish one's faith in the value of athletic activities as a social outing. And anyone who does not take the time, while in Japan, to watch and learn about sumo wrestling is missing an enormous opportunity to get into the heart and soul of the country.

What follows relates primarily to the business setting and to professional considerations. But do take advantage of your time in Japan to explore the depth and diversity of this wonderful country and people. The knowledge and insight gained into the Japanese will only add to the benefits of a working trip to Japan.

Business Accommodations

Most business travelers to Japan opt for the larger Western style "international" hotels. Although very expensive, these hotels have all the necessary business amenities and staff who speak English, both important advantages. In addition, if you are going to be

A Ryokan, or a traditional Japanese inn, is one way to experience the richness of Japanese culture. A dinner, like the one shown here, is often part of the Ryokan experience.

picked up or dropped off at your hotel, an up-scale hotel is the best choice as it projects the right image. If you are on a small budget, business hotels are considerably less expensive (one-half or one-third of the price). They tend to be located conveniently near train stations but, although clean and respectable, have few business facilities.

Other options include capsule hotels (which are inexpensive as you only get a tiny room—even by Japanese standards—a television and little else) and traditional *ryokan* (Japanese inns), which vary dramatically in style and price. Your room in a *ryokan* will be a Japanese *tatami* room with sliding screen doors and basic furniture. Breakfast and dinner are usually included in your room charge and served in your room. More information can be obtained from the Japan National Tourist Organization's (JNTO) publications: the *Japan Hotel Guide* and the *Japan Ryokan Guide*. The JNTO can be contacted in the United States or Canada at:

JNTO United States
Suite 2101
630 Fifth Avenue
New York, NY 10111
Tel: 212 757-5640

JNTO Canada
165 University Avenue
Toronto, Ontario
M5H 3B8
Tel: 416 366-7140

or through their web site at http://www/jnto.go.jp/index.html
Further hotel information can be obtained by checking the web
sites listed in the reference section at the end of the book.

Culture of Cash

Japan relies heavily on cash. Credit cards can be used in major
hotels and restaurants, but business travelers heading away from
major centers should carry a sizable amount of cash. Travelers
cheques can be cashed at most banks, but be warned that the
process can take a fairly long time—tellers do not have a great
deal of experience in dealing with foreigners. Most travelers try
to cash their travelers cheques at their hotels.

There are very few cash machines available in the country. It is
quite amusing (unless you are the one caught in this dilemma) to
watch visitors, credit card in hand, cruising the streets in a desperate
attempt to find a terminal that will accept their cards. The Japanese
banks do not offer access—you will have to find a Citibank outlet.
(There is one near the main intersection in Ropongi—down a small
side alley—and another in the Shibuya district—exit by the famous
dog statue, turn left and go along for about two blocks.) The sheer
delight that comes from having successfully tracked down a friendly
banking terminal after a half-day search through the city has to be
experienced to be fully understood.

Incidentally, for a nation of determined savers and cash-
carrying business people and travelers, the Japanese have a lot of
plastic. There are well over 200,000 million credit cards in
circulation—not bad for a country of 125 million people—but
most Japanese still rely heavily on cash for payment.

Eating Out in Japan

There are many different types of restaurants in Japan from the very casual and inexpensive to the elegant and astronomically expensive. Guidebooks can give you suggestions of restaurants to try, and there are a couple of books just on dining in Japan that introduce you to and show you pictures of a wide range of Japanese foods. English language magazines like the *Tokyo Journal* or the *Tokyo Weekender* (for the Tokyo area), or *Kansai Time-out* (for the Osaka, Kyoto, and Kobe area) are good for recommending ethnic restaurants. (Check the reference section for their web sites.) If you are wandering around downtown, try the top floor of most department stores for a reasonable cross section of mid-range restaurants.

Unlike Japanese restaurants outside of Japan where you can get a wide range of Japanese foods, most restaurants in Japan usually serve only one type of food. A sushi restaurant will serve almost exclusively sushi, and you will not be able to get *yakitori* (grilled chicken) or *ramen* noodles there.

Most restaurants have a big display case outside filled with plastic models of the various foods that the restaurant serves and their prices (usually in Arabic numbers but occasionally in Japanese numbers). These models are incredibly detailed and, in most cases, the meal that you order looks *exactly* like the model, right down to the garnish! Looking at the plastic models should help you decide if the restaurant serves what you want. The display case often shows everything that the restaurant serves so if it isn't there, the odds are that the restaurant doesn't make it. If you see a plastic model of a meal that you want but don't know what it is called in Japanese, you can always take the waitress outside and point it out.

Noodles

The Japanese have a number of varieties of noodles (*soba, udon, ramen, somen*), and you will find noodle shops all over Japan. Noodles are most commonly found in hot soups with pieces of meat, vegetables, shrimp tempura, or other such things on top. You will also come across a fried noodle dish called *yakisoba* (*yaki* means "to cook"), which consists of fried soba noodles with vegetables, meat (usually pork), and ginger in a tasty sauce. This is an inexpensive dish sold as a snack at outdoor fairs and in convenience stores, as well as in noodle restaurants. Sometimes, noodles are served cold with a broth to dip them in (not pour over them as the bamboo mat on which they are served does not hold liquid!).

Sushi

Today, sushi is a popular delicacy in many countries. There are a few varieties of what is collectively referred to as sushi. *Nigiri sushi* consists of raw or cooked fish or seafood on delicately flavored blocks of rice. In *maki sushi*, rice and vegetables or fish are rolled up in a sheet of *nori* (seaweed) and then cut into small pieces. *Sashimi* is the raw fish served by itself, not on the rice.

Sushi bars differ in quality and price. At the low end are places where the sushi is placed on a conveyer belt that goes around in a circle. Customers choose the types of sushi they want and, at the end, an employee tallies up the cost by the number and plate types. (Some types of sushi cost more and are placed on different plates.) Other sushi bars are exquisite in every detail, from the decor to the service to the quality of each and every ingredient. These places naturally tend to be very expensive.

Sushi is usually served in twos with slices of pink ginger. You are supposed to eat a piece of ginger before the sushi, and between different types of sushi, to cleanse your palate. *Wasabi*, the green Japanese horseradish, is already applied to nigiri sushi. You will be given a small dish to which you could add *shoyu* (soya sauce) and wasabi. You then dip your sushi in the soya sauce. You should turn the sushi over so that you are dipping the fish, not the rice. This way the rice doesn't dissolve in the sauce. You can use your hands or your chopsticks when eating sushi.

It is also easier to eat the entire piece of sushi at one go rather than trying to nibble at it. If you can't face the thought of raw fish, try *ebi* (shrimp, usually cooked), *tamago* (egg), *kyuri* (cucumber in *kappa maki*) or *unagi* (broiled eel). *Maguro* is raw tuna, but the taste is very mild and good. Your Japanese hosts will want to give you what you want, so mention the types that you like (without mentioning what you don't like), and they will be sure to serve you those.

Teishoku

Certain restaurants serve or give you the option of a *teishoku* meal. Teishoku is a complete meal, including a main dish, soup, rice, and a small dish of pickles all on one tray. The main dish might be *tempura* (lightly deep fried vegetables and/or prawns) or *tonkatsu* (a breaded deep fried pork cutlet) or teriyaki chicken or a variety of other choices.

In any big Japanese city, there will be a number of Western fast-food restaurants like McDonald's, Mister Donuts, and Kentucky Fried Chicken. If you crave coffee and don't want to spend a fortune, there are a couple of inexpensive coffee shops chains scattered all over Japan. Doutors coffee shops are probably the most common so keep an eye out for them, and enjoy a cup of coffee for a couple of hundred yen. Starbucks, the Seattle coffee chain, even has a couple of outlets in Tokyo now! There are also many of what the Japanese refer to as "family restaurants" like Dennys and Royal Host where you can sample a range of Western-style foods like steaks, spaghetti, pizza, and salads. All of these restaurants have big plastic menus with lots of color photographs, and the names of the various dishes are often listed in English as well as in Japanese.

In major Japanese cities, you can find food from a wide range of ethnic restaurants, from Indian to Mexican, Thai, Russian, Ghanian, Peruvian, and Spanish just to name a few. Yokohama has a famous Chinatown that is well worth a visit, and there are Chinese restaurants in most Japanese cities of any size.

Dining Etiquette

Dining together is a significant part of Japanese protocol. Make plans to dine with your Japanese counterparts on your first evening out in Japan. You may also wish to host a dinner but be prepared for a large bill. Get suggestions from your hosts or other Japanese friends on the choice of restaurant.

Although your Japanese hosts will not necessarily expect you to be comfortable with chopsticks, it is probably worth your while to spend some time practicing with them before you go to Japan. To use chopsticks correctly, the lower chopstick should be held still while the upper chopstick, held between the thumb and the index and middle fingers, is moved up and down. Don't worry if you don't use chopsticks perfectly—being willing to try is most important.

At almost all restaurants, the first thing you will receive is a hot damp cloth called *o-shibori*. This is used to wash your hands (sometimes men also wash their faces) and refresh yourself before the meal begins. Fold up your cloth when you are done.

In many Japanese restaurants (not Western-style ones), you will be seated on tatami mats at a low table. *O-cha* (Japanese green tea) will be served before or after the meal. There is no extra charge for this, and your cup will be continually refilled. O-cha is drunk without milk or sugar.

Pub-style restaurants often serve a small dish of peas or a type of appetizer at around the time your drinks are served. There is no charge for this, and it is often called a *chaamu* (from the English word "charm").

Some General Rules

- Do not fidget or gesture with your chopsticks before or during a meal.
- Do not stick chopsticks vertically in your rice when pausing between courses. (This is a way of offering rice to the dead.)

- Do not pour soya sauce directly on your rice. Rice is meant to be eaten plain.
- Do not take food off a serving dish using your own chopsticks unless you turn them around and use the ends that have not been in your mouth. If serving chopsticks are available, use those.
- It is acceptable (more for men than for women) to slurp slightly when eating noodles or drinking tea. It is a sign of appreciation.
- Use both hands when drinking tea or soup.
- It is good manners to bring bowls to your mouth level when eating. It is impolite to leave the rice bowl on the table when eating.
- Put lids back on bowls when you have finished eating.
- All courses in a Japanese set meal are served at once, including the soup. The soup should not be gulped down before eating the other courses. Everything should be eaten a little at a time.
- Do not blow your nose at the table.
- You do not need to tip in Japanese restaurants. A service charge is added to some hotel and restaurant bills.

Finding a Restaurant in Japan

Here are a few hints. The area around most major subway stations includes a sizable shopping and restaurant district. In the mazes of back roads and side streets around the stations, there are often dozens of little restaurants. Remember that there is no one menu that is typically Japanese. The country boasts a variety of regional and cultural specialties.

Within a few blocks, you will often find a horrifically expensive Japanese restaurant serving a gourmet meal ($400 plus for four), a McDonald's or two, several inexpensive Japanese restaurants and, in the larger centers, those serving food from other countries and cultures. Many of these restaurants are located on upper floors, and most make no effort whatsoever to cater to foreigners. Signs are typically in *kanji* and are difficult to understand. Ask the locals for advice—and a map.

A final note: if you are in a busy restaurant during lunch hour, do not be surprised if the waiter sits someone next to you. In restaurants, as everywhere else in Japan, space is at a premium.

Entertaining

Socializing after hours is a significant part of doing business in Japan, particularly for men. Going out drinking whether it is with colleagues, customers, bosses, or subordinates builds up trust and rapport and strengthens the working relationship. If you are invited to join your business colleagues in an evening out drinking or at a *karaoke* bar (the literal meaning is "empty orchestra," but it refers to a bar with a microphone and video monitor that allows you to sing along to your favorite songs), you would be wise to go. Drinking evenings are not a time to discuss business but an opportunity to relax and get to know each other. Diana Rowland, in *Japanese Business Etiquette* describes the importance of these drinking evenings:

> "For the Japanese male, social drinking is an outlet. At the heart of this ritual is the old inflexible, unwritten law that surface harmony must be maintained at all costs. Naturally, this is very stressful, as one must constantly suppress his emotions and opinions for the sake of group harmony.
>
> Intoxication is the time, or the state, in which a Japanese man can express himself rather freely and with impunity—an opportunity to show his true nature without fear of repercussion. It is a time of "intermission" when many of the rules of etiquette go out the window and the normal restrictive rules of behavior don't apply.
>
> Getting drunk, or at least giving the appearance of it, is not only condoned, it is actually encouraged as a means of bonding. The Japanese will proceed to sing, laugh, even dance and play in such a totally uninhibited manner that it may seem childlike to the circumspect Western businessman." (p 126)

Much of what occurs during a night of drinking is easily forgiven, and these evenings provide an opportunity for people to express thoughts or grievances that they could never otherwise mention. However, be careful to never refer back to things that happened or were said during a drinking evening. Do, however, remember to say "thank you" for the evening the next time you see your colleagues.

There is a certain etiquette to drinking just as there is to dining. You never pour your own beer or sake. Your host or the person sitting beside you will do it for you. You do, however, pour drinks for the people seated near you. Beer or sake is ordered for the whole group so you can pick up any bottle and pour it for anyone at the table. When someone is pouring the drink for you, you should lift your glass. Women tend to hold their glass with both hands (one hand underneath the glass), while men hold with one unless pouring for someone of higher rank. If heading to a karaoke bar, you would be well advised to have prepared one or two songs that you will feel comfortable singing. The Japanese like to get everyone involved in karaoke, and it can appear rude and unfriendly to decline an offer to do so.

When you have had enough to drink, just keep your glass full. This keeps it from being refilled. If you do not drink at all, mention this at the outset. To avoid any questions, indicate that you have a medical condition that does not allow you to drink. Orange juice, soft drinks, and oolong tea are served at most places so you can drink those instead. Do not be surprised if your entire meal and evening's entertainment occurs without any input from you.

For foreign business women, Japanese after-dinner socializing can be fraught with difficulties. In *Doing Business with Japanese Men*, Christalynn Brannen and Tracey Wilen explain to their women readers why:

> "Because while these same men are discussing business or just getting to know each other, they are in an atmosphere where you would feel completely out of place. These small eateries, pubs, karaoke bars, hostess clubs, and other nightspots are designed exclusively for the entertainment of men. The women who work there may be scantily clad liquor servers, or kimono-clad hostesses whose job it is to fawn over the men, light their cigarettes, keep their glasses full, and engage in suggestive sexual banter. Some are certainly prostitutes." (p 73)

What the Business Person Should Know

National Holidays in Japan

January 1	*Shogatsu*	New Year's Day
January 15	*Seijin-no-hi*	Coming-of-Age Day
February 11	*Kenkoku-kinen-no-hi*	National Founding Day
March 20	*Shunbun-no-hi*	Vernal Equinox
April 29	*Midori-no-hi*	Greenery Day
May 3	*Kenpo-kinenbi*	Constitution Memorial Day
May 5	*Kodomo-no-hi*	Children's Day or Boys' Festival
July 20	*Umi-no-hi*	Marine Day
September 15	*Keiro-no-hi*	Respect for the Aged Day
September 23	*Shuubun-no-hi*	Autumnal Equinox
October 10	*Taiiku-no-hi*	Health-Sports Day
November 3	*Bunka-no-hi*	Culture Day
November 23	*Kinro-kansha-no-hi*	Labor Thanksgiving Day
December 23	*Tenno-tanjobi*	Emperor's Birthday

- When a national holiday falls on a Sunday, the following Monday becomes a holiday.
- A day sandwiched by national holidays (excluding the case in which it falls on a Sunday of any of the holidays above) becomes a holiday.

Major Annual Long Vacations
(for White-Collar Workers in Urban Areas)

Year-end and New Year's Day holidays: Civil servants usually end work on December 28 and return to work on January 4.

"Golden Week": April 29 to around May 5.

"Bon" Festival holidays: Around August 15 (or July 15 according to the lunar calendar).

Summer holidays: Mostly concentrated in July and August, but people traveling abroad often take their holiday in late August when air fares are cheaper.

Source: Savoe, *Jetro, Nippon 1997: Business Facts and Figures*. (Tokyo: Jetro, 1997), p 160.

Brannen and Wiley suggest that many women are likely to find the bar/club scene somewhere between uncomfortable and insulting and, they suggest, participating could even make you less effective in your business dealings. Bowing out after dinner is the best solution and easily managed as dinner and the drinking occur in different places, they suggest. Brannen and Wiley do say though that many of the foreign business women they interviewed "felt it was perfectly okay to socialize with their Japanese clients. They said that, although they left a bit earlier than the men on their team, they felt that there was no disadvantage to joining in on the night-time entertainment." (p 74) Obviously then, each woman will have to decide herself whether or not to participate and, if so, to what extent.

Getting Around Japan

The first challenge you are likely to face when arriving in Japan is getting from Narita airport to Tokyo. If you are doing business in Osaka or Nagoya and can arrange your flights and meetings so that you arrive in one of those cities, that would be a good move. Narita airport is often very busy, and it is a considerable distance from Tokyo. This means that after your long flight you are faced with crowded lines through customs and immigration and then a long bus or train ride into the city. If you arrive in Osaka or, particularly. Nagoya, these hassles are greatly diminished.

To get to downtown Tokyo from Narita, you can take the limousine bus that stops at most of the major hotels in Tokyo. You buy your ticket from a clearly marked booth in the arrival area. If you are not staying at a major hotel, find out what train station or major hotel is near your accommodations.

Getting the place you will be staying to fax you a map is always useful. Because Tokyo is a very confusing maze-like city, most offices and hotels have maps that they fax out to help people find them. Show the people at the limousine bus booth your map and ask them what bus you should take (various limousine buses take different routes) and at what hotel you should get off. The limousine bus will cost about 3,000 yen, depending on your destination. A limousine bus goes on each route once or twice an hour. On arriving at the hotel, depending on distances and finances, you can then take a taxi or the subway to your accommodations.

Your other option is to take either the Japan Railways Narita Express train or the Keisei Railways Skyliner limited express trains directly from an underground level of the Narita terminal building. The Narita Express goes to five main train stations (Yokohama, Tokyo, Shinjuku, Ofuna, and Ikebukuro), and the journey takes between 60 and 90 minutes and costs approximately 3500 yen. The Skyliner goes to the Nippori and Keisei-Ueno stations in 55 and 60 minutes respectively and costs between 1500 and 2000 yen.

If you have to transfer to a domestic flight that leaves from Haneda airport, there is the Airport Limited Express, which links Narita with Haneda airport in about 1 hour 45 minutes without the inconvenience of changing trains.

For travel within Tokyo or the Kansai (Osaka area), pick up a map of the subway and train system. Maps in English are available at the bigger train stations. In bigger Japanese cities, taking the subway and the train is usually faster and more efficient than taking a cab or going by car. The subway and the trains run frequently between approximately 5 a.m. and midnight. Morning and evening rush hours, particularly on certain routes like the Yamanote line that does a loop in central Tokyo, can be incredibly crowded even though trains run about every two minutes!!

Buses also run in many areas. The payment system varies by location. In Tokyo, you usually pay a set fare upon entering the bus. In other areas, when you get on (at the front or in the middle of the bus), you take a slip of paper with a number on it. An electronic sign at the front of the bus displays the number and the corresponding charge that increases the longer you stay on the bus. You deposit the amount indicated underneath your number when you disembark.

Taxi stands can be found at most train stations. Alternatively, you can hail a cab on the street. There are two sizes of cabs and two starting prices. There is an additional charge for cabs after 11 p.m. and before 5 a.m. Taxis in Japan are usually very clean, and the drivers often wear white gloves. The driver opens and closes the back passenger door with a lever so do not attempt to open or close that door yourself. It can be extremely difficult to find your way around a big Japanese city even for taxi drivers. So it is important that you have a map to your destination or, at the very least, the address written out clearly in Japanese. You do not need to tip taxi drivers.

For information on travel within Japan, visit the Japan Railways information office in Tokyo station. You can also call JR's English Language Telephone Service, which provides information in English on train times, schedules, fares, and recommended routings. The office is open Monday to Friday (except holidays) from 10 a.m. until 6 p.m. The phone number is (03) 3423-0111.

If you are planning on doing a considerable amount of travel within Japan, it would be worth considering a Japan Rail Pass. Passes for 7, 14, and 21 days are available and, although not cheap, are a good deal. One round trip between Tokyo and Kyoto costs slightly less than the one week pass. If you plan on doing any more traveling than that, the pass would be worth it. The one catch with the Japan Rail Pass is that you must purchase it outside the country, and you must be on a tourist visa. When you begin using your pass, you are required to take it to the JR information office in Tokyo station, where they will check your passport, take your ticket voucher, and give you a small booklet with the first day of the pass stamped. For further information on travel and accommodations in Japan, check out the reading and web sites listed in the reference section.

Japanese Language

Japanese is written using a mixture of *kanji*, *hiragana*, and *katakana*. Kanji are ideograms or characters. They were invented by the Chinese who basically began writing by drawing pictures of things that they knew. Gradually, they modified these pictures into a writing system by simplifying and adjusting the pictures so that they would be similar sizes and would all fit into a square. Until about the third century A.D., the Japanese did not have any form of written language so they borrowed the Chinese writing system. The Japanese took the Chinese written characters and matched them with the equivalent spoken word in Japanese. If the Japanese did not have a spoken word to match, they borrowed the Chinese pronunciation along with the written character.

Linguistically, however, the Japanese and Chinese languages are very different. As Len Walsh explains in *Read Japanese Today* about written Japanese:

> "While the Japanese could use these imported Chinese characters to write the basic roots of words, they could not use them to write the grammatical endings because Japanese grammar and morphology were so different from the Chinese. In Chinese there were no grammatical endings to show what part of speech a word is (corresponding in English to ending such as *-tion*, *-ish*, *-ed*, and to such auxiliary words as *had been*, *will be*, *could* and *would*) but in Japanese there were." (p 17)

Initially, the Japanese tried to use the Chinese characters to write the roots and the grammatical endings, but they discovered that this did not work too well. Eventually, they decided to abbreviate some of the characters into a kind of alphabet, a phonetic system that would let them write the necessary grammatical endings. They called this phonetic system *kana*. Now, Japanese is written with the word roots (it does not matter if the word is a noun, an adjective, or a verb) in kanji and the grammatical endings written in kana. It is easy to tell the characters from the kana because while kana are written with two to four separate lines or strokes, the kanji have a minimum of two strokes (with the exception of the character for "one," which consists of one line) but are usually composed of many strokes.

There are two kinds of kana: *hiragana* and *katakana*. Hiragana is the regular "alphabet," while katakana is used for words borrowed from foreign languages and for foreign names. Kana are syllables, and the basic units of Japanese pronunciation.

Those interested in studying Japanese seriously will want to find a class in their area. Those who are not planning on studying Japanese seriously may not be interested in learning the writing system, but knowledge of the syllables and their pronunciation will help you pronounce Japanese names and the basic vocabulary listed below. When Japanese words are written using the English alphabet, this is called *roomaji*. Below is a list of the basic Japanese sounds in roomaji:

AH	WE	SOON	GET	OLD
a	i	u	e	o
ka	ki	ku	ke	ko
sa	shi	su	se	so
ta	chi	tsu	te	to
na	ni	nu	ne	no
ha	hi	fu	he	ho
ma	mi	mu	me	mo
ya		yu		yo
ra	ri	ru	re	ro
wa				wo
ga	gi	gu	ge	go
za	ji	zu	ze	zo
da			de	do
ba	bi	bu	be	bo
pa	pi	pu	pe	po
n				

Please note that the sounds below the columns "Ah, we soon get old" do not lament the aging process but are a guideline for pronouncing each of the basic Japanese sounds.

Most Japanese pronunciation is quite similar to English. One exception is "r," which is softer than the English "r"—somewhere between and "r" and an "l." (The Japanese only have the one sound, which is why Japanese often have difficulty distinguishing between "r" and "l" in English.) Most Japanese words are said with equal emphasis on each syllable.

There are some words with either double vowels (aa, ii, ee, oo, uu) or double consonants (pp, kk, ss, ssh, tt). When there is a double vowel (like in roomaji above or in the city name Oosaka), each vowel is pronounced. The double vowel is sometimes written as above with the two vowels and sometimes with one vowel with a line over it. As words with a double vowel mean something entirely different from those with a single vowel (e.g. ob*asan* means "aunt," while ob*aa*san means grandmother), proper pronunciation is essential. Double consonants in words like Roppongi (the disco area in central Tokyo), Hokkaido (Japan's northern most main island), or Beppu (a city in southern Japan) also must be noted. The first consonant is given the same emphasis as a full syllable.

Some Basic Expressions

Greetings

Good Morning	Ohayoo gozaimasu
Good Afternoon	Konnichi wa
Good Evening	Konban wa
Good Night	Oyasumi Nasai
Good-bye	Sayoonara
This is Mr./Mrs./Miss/Ms …	Kochira wa … san desu
I'm pleased to meet you.	Hajimemashite
Yes (thanks to you)	Ee. O-kage sama de

Other Useful Expressions:

I understand	Wakarimasu
I don't understand	Wakarimasen
Thank you	Arigatoo
Thank you very much	Doomo arigatoo gozaimasu
Thank you (for food or drink) (e.g. when someone gives you a treat)	Gochisosama deshita
You are welcome	Doo itashimashite
Please (when offering something)	Dozo
Please (when requesting)	Onegai shimasu
Excuse me	Sumimasen
I am sorry	Gomen nasai
Cheers	Kanpai

Question Words:

Where?	Doko
Where is/are …?	… wa doko desu ka?
When?	Itsu
What?	Nani
How much?	Ikura
How much does it cost?	Ikura desu ka
Who?	Dare
Why?	Naze

Settling Down in Japan

For those planning to stay in Japan for awhile, there are many different challenges to simply settling in. If you are sponsored by a Japanese or foreign company or are going to Japan on the Japan

Exchange Teachers Program (JET), which brings several hundred foreign teachers to Japan to work as assistant English teachers in Japanese schools, you will likely have someone who will be able to help you with some of these hurdles.

If you are considering going to Japan to look for work or to start a business, then you are much more on your own. What follows is an overview of some of the most important information you will need to know. Again, please refer to the web sites listed at the end, and spend some time exploring them. There are a number of sites put together by foreigners living in, or just back from, Japan who discuss their experiences and the information they wish they had known before arriving in Japan. These anecdotal sites are well worth reading.

Inside the Japanese Household

Japanese households are small by international standards, and many foreigners are amazed at the cramped conditions of the average house or apartment. Recognizing the limitations of space, Japanese firms have been creative in creating products that use a minimal amount of space. For example, many Japanese bathrooms are one-piece units with a shower, toilet bowl, and sink.

At the same time, the Japanese are enthusiastic consumers and rush to the stores to try out new products. According to 1996 statistics, virtually all Japanese homes have color television sets, washing machines, refrigerators, and vacuum cleaners. Over 80% have cars and microwave ovens. Many homes have video cassette recorders or VCRs (74%), compact disc players (57%), stereos (58%), and airconditioning (77%). Over 30% have satellite receivers and video cameras.

It is a wonder that they mange to fit all these things into the small apartments, but it is worth noting that Japanese families rarely keep second-hand or even outdated equipment. Appliances are replaced often, and the used equipment is simply thrown away. (This is why it is easy to furnish your home on "big garbage day," a time when households are permitted to dispose of large unwanted items. Foreigners have less compunction than the Japanese in picking up other people's unwanted goods — they may, in fact, find many useful, functional appliances and furniture pieces.)

Accommodations

Searching for a place to live in Japan can be a real hassle. There are real estate agents who cater to foreigners, but the accommodation they propose is usually very expensive. The advertisements in the *Japan Times* newspaper are also primarily for expensive properties. The type of accommodations you need or can afford will depend a great deal on your budget.

For those on a smaller budget, there are some places to stay temporarily that are relatively inexpensive. *Gaijin* (foreigner) houses can be found in Tokyo. These are shared homes populated primarily by non-Japanese, and they range in price and cleanliness! "Weekly mansions" is another option. Do not let the mansion part fool you! These are very small, furnished (bed that folds down from the wall, television, phone, bathroom, half-sized fridge, one burner) apartments that can be rented by the week. As it can be difficult to find reasonably priced short-term accommodation, a "weekly mansion" might be suitable while you search for something more long term.

When you rent in Japan, there are a number of extra charges to take into account. It is not unheard of to be required to pay, before you move in, your first month's rent as commission to the *fudosan* (real estate agent), two months' rent as a *shikikin* (deposit), and another two months' rent as a *reikin* (non-refundable deposit or key money). You will not get much of this money back. You will also need a guarantor to get the apartment, either someone from your company or a friend.

Alien Registration

Within 90 days of your arrival in Japan, you must apply for an alien registration card at your local municipal office. You will need your passport and two 4.5 cm by 3.5 cm photographs of yourself.

Driver's License

International driver's licenses are valid for one year from the date

Hotel prices in major Japanese cities can be very expensive. Visitors planning on staying longer could rent a room in one of the many "weekly mansions" available.

of issue. After that or if you do not have an international license, you must get one from the local motor vehicle branch. You need a photograph, alien registration card, passport, foreign driver's license and a translation of it (in larger centers the translation might not be needed if the original license is in Chinese, Korean, or English, but it might not be worth risking going without it), and will be asked to pay a small handling charge. You may have to take an eye test and/or attend a safety demonstration.

Medical Information

If you cannot find a doctor when you are ill or injured, call the Tokyo Metropolitan Health and Medical Information Center at (03) 5285-8181 or the AMDA Medical Information Service at (03) 5285-8088. Both centers are open from 9 a.m. to 5 p.m. on weekdays and offer services in English, Chinese, Korean, Thai, and Spanish, as well as other in other languages at selected times. A 24-hour service is available in Japanese at (03) 5272-0303. For foreign patients in hospitals, interpretation services by phone are available at (03) 5285-8185 between 5 p.m. and 10 p.m. on weekdays and 9 p.m. and 10 p.m. on weekends and holidays. In an emergency, dial 119.

Medical insurance is highly recommended. For the first year, you can probably get by on travel insurance bought in your home country, but after that you will want some Japanese insurance. If you do not get insurance through your work, go to your local ward office and apply for national health insurance.

Visas

Check the immigration requirements for your particular country. Citizens of many countries can stay in Japan for ninety days without a visa. Longer than ninety days and a different kind of visa is required. Australian, Canadian, and New Zealand citizens below the age of 30 (varies by country) can apply for a "working holiday" visa before they leave their home country. This visa is designed to give young people a chance to travel and work to support themselves for a period of six months to one year.

If you enter Japan on a tourist visa and then find a job while you are there, you must leave the country to have the visa processed at a Japanese consulate abroad. You must also be sponsored (someone takes responsibility for you while you are in Japan) by your employer. Working visas can be harder to obtain for people without university degrees. Student visas are available for studying full-time at language schools and cultural visas can be obtained for the study of some aspect of Japanese culture like *ikebana* (flower arranging), *karate*, or *kendo*.

This chapter, by no means, provides an exhaustive list of Japanese culture and lifestyle. There are a series of excellent books and guides that provide very specific information on some aspects of Japan. Japan is still seen by many foreigners as a very mysterious and even strange place. And "old hands" love to tell stories about unusual meals, getting lost in Tokyo, and other difficulties encountered by foreigners. Take all these stories with a grain of salt. The Japan of twenty years ago no longer exists. The country is well-used to tourists and business people and is sufficiently Westernized that you can find numerous familiar sights, sounds, and tastes. Japan works, despite some outward appearances of being crowded, chaotic, and disorganized. And it is sufficiently friendly that even the most unilingual foreigner will receive ample help in navigating the shoals of Japanese cities and culture.

More than anything—and particularly if you hope to develop long-term business relationships in the country—visiting business people should take the time to experience Japan and should avoid the standard temptation to shy away from its unique characteristics. You might not have angler fish livers high on your list of dining favorites, but do give them a try. And if you learn a bit about sumo; take in a baseball game; go to Japanese theatre; visit a shrine or temple; shop at a local market; travel on the subways and commuter trains; flip through a *manga* (comic) at a newsstand or bookstore or visit Tokyo's Harajuku district; spend some time at the Shibuya and Shinjuku stations (two of the largest such commuter centres in the world); visit the memorials in Hiroshima and Nagasaki; walk through the reconstructed sections of Kobe; and go on a quiet weekend hike in the park with ten or fifteen thousand other walkers, you will, gradually and with delight, come to better understand Japan.

Do the above things for the immense personal benefits that come from such learning and experiences, but realize that this may be the most important set of activities you undertake as someone seeking to do business in Japan. For in Japan, like in most countries, learning about the culture and people of the country is the best foundation for business success.

Directory of Important Contacts

Telephone Operator Speaks English (*)
International Office within the Organization (**)
English-Speaking Staff Available (***)

All Japan International Traders
Federation
3563-1786 **

Asian Affairs Research Council
3211-1616 ***

Assoc. for Promotion of
International Trade (Japan)
3506-8261 ***

BIAC Japan (OECD)
3279-1411 **

Defense Agency, Govt of Japan
3408-5211 **

Economic Planning Agency,
Govt of Japan
3581-0261 **

Environment Agency,
Govt of Japan
3581-3351 ***

Federation of Bankers Assoc.
of Japan
3216-3761 **

Food Agency, Govt of Japan
3501-8111 **

Industry Club of Japan
3281-1711 ***

Industry of Developing
Economies
3353-4231

Institute of World Economy
5484-3346 ***

Institute for Int. Trade and
Investments (ITI)
5563-1251 *

International Assoc. for the
Protection of Industrial
Property
3591-5301 *

International Chamber of
Commerce (ICC-Japan)
3213-8585 *

International Management Association of Japan, Inc.
3502-3051 *

Japan Centre for Economic Research
3639-2801 ***

Japan Iron and Steel Federation
3279-3611

Japan Securities Dealers Association
3667-8451 **

Japan Science Foundation
3212-8471 ***

Japan Federation of Economic Organizations (Keidanren)
3279-1411 **

Japan Federation of Employers' Associations (Nikkeiren)
3213-4474

Japan Assoc. of Corporate Executives (Keizai Doyukai)
3211-1271 ***

Japan Patent Association
3206-2241

Japan Productivity Center for Socio-Economic Development
3409-1111 *

Japan Marketing Association
3403-5101 ***

Japan Management Association
3434-6211 **

Japan Economic Research Institute
3214-0541 ***

Japan Institute of Invention and Innovation
3502-5421

Japan Foreign Trade Council, Inc.
3435-5952 **

Japan Federation of Smaller Enterprise Organization
3668-2481

Japan External Trade Organization (JETRO)
3582-5522 **

Japan Consumers Association
3553-8601

Japan Chamber of Commerce and Industry
3282-7823 *

Japan Association for Trade with Russia and Cen-Eastern Europe
3551-6215 *

Japan-China Association on Economy and Trade
3402-1981 ***

Japan-Commercial Arbitration Association
3287-3051 ***

Japanese Institute of Certified Public Accountants
3818-5551 **

Japanese Standards Association
3583-8005 **

Kansai Assoc. of Corporate Executives (Kansai Keizai Doyukai)
06-441-1031 ***

Life Insurance Association of Japan
3286-2624 **

Manufactured Imports Promotion Organization (MIPRO)
3988-2791 *

Marine and Fire Insurance Association of Japan, Inc.
3255-1211 **

Ministry of Construction, Govt of Japan
3580-4311 **

Ministry of Finance, Govt of Japan
3581-4111 *

Ministry of Justice, Govt of Japan
3580-4111 **

Ministry of Foreign Affairs, Govt of Japan
3580-3311 *

Ministry of Education, Govt of Japan
3581-4211 **

Ministry of Labor, Govt of Japan
3593-1211 **

Ministry of Health and Welfare, Govt of Japan
3503-1711 **

Ministry of Agriculture, Forestry and Fisheries, Govt of Japan
3502-8111 **

Ministry of International Trade and Industry, Govt of Japan
3501-1511 **

Ministry of Posts & Telecommunications, Govt of Japan
3504-4411 **

Ministry of Transport, Govt of Japan
3580-3111 **

Ministry of Home Affairs. Govt of Japan
3581-5311 ***

National Tax Administration Agency, Govt of Japan
3581-5161 **

National Federation of Small Business Associations
3586-2627

**Osaka Foreign Trade
Association**
06-942-2701, ext. 7677

Patent Office, Govt of Japan
3581-1101 **

**Science and Technology
Agency, Govt of Japan**
3581-5271 **

**Tokyo Commodity Exchange for
Industry**
3661-9191 ***

**Tokyo Foreign Trade
Association**
3438-2026 ***

Tokyo Grain Exchange
3668-9311 ***

**Tokyo International Trade Fair
Commission**
5530-1111 ***

Tokyo Stock Exchange
3666-0141 **

**Tokyo Chamber of Commerce
and Industry**
3282-7580 **

World Trade Center Japan, Inc.
3435-5657 *

Source: JETRO, Nippon, 1998
(Tokyo: JETRO, 1997), p. 160.

Recommended Reading

The library of books on Japan, the Japanese economy, and Japanese business is enormous and wide-ranging. At times, writers have marveled at the Japanese "miracle" and have struggled to interpret this economic phenomena to outsiders. On other occasions, as over the last few years, many writers have assumed that the period of Japanese success was nearing the end, and have written more pessimistic forecasts and analyses. The following list consists of those books that we feel best explore the complexity:

Brannen, Christalyn and Tracey Wilen, *Doing Business With Japanese Men: A Woman's Handbook* (Stone Bridge Press, 1993). An insightful guide into the unique challenges of being a foreign woman working in Japan.

Czinkota, M. and Jon Woronoff, *Unlocking Japan's Markets: Seizing Marketing and Distribution Opportunities in Today's Japan* (Tokyo: Tuttle, 1993). A critical and useful investigation of the inner workings of the Japanese business system, with some helpful suggestions on how to capitalize on emerging opportunities.

Dore, Ronald, *Taking Japan Seriously; A Confucian Perspective on Leading Economic Issues* (London: Athlone, 1987). This book provides helpful cultural insights into the structure and ethos of the Japanese business environment.

Emmot, Bill, *Japan's Global Reach: The Influences, Strategies and Weaknesses of Japan's Multinational Companies* (New York: Arrow, 1993). Emmot provides an important investigation into the international activities of some of Japan's largest corporations. Events have changed the situation he describes, but these companies remain very influential in Japan and in international trade.

Engholm, Christopher, *When Business East Meets Business West: The Guide to Practise and Protocol in the Pacific Rim* (New York: John Wiley and Sons, 1991). This volume provides useful practical advise on observing cultural norms and responding to Asian expectations.

Fallows, James, *Looking at the Sun: The Rise of The New East Asian Economic and Political System* (New York: Vintage, 1995). This is an insightful and optimistic account (somewhat overrun by the turn of events) of the emerging power of Japan and East Asia.

Fields, George, *From Bonzai to Levis* (New York: Signet, 1985). A classic on the opportunities, successes and foibles of foreign businesses attempting to enter the Japanese market.

Fingleton, Eamonn, *Blindside — Why Japan is Still On Track to Overtake the U.S. By the Year* 2000 (New York: Buttonwood Press, 1995). Fingleton offers a strong and controversial voice on the nature and future progress of the Japanese economy. He does not support the argument that Japan is facing long-term economic difficulties and instead argues that the country's business community and economy is actually doing surprisingly well.

Hartcher, Peter, *The Ministry: How Japan's Most Powerful Institution Endangers World Market* (Boston: Harvard School Business Press, 1998). For many years, observers assumed that the Ministry of International Trade and Industry "ran" the Japanese economy. Hartcher and others argue that the Ministry of Finance is actually the power behind Japan's commercial success—and the agency responsible for the country's current economic distress.

Heenan, Patrick, ed., *The Japan Handbook* (London: Fitzroy Dearborn, 1998). This book is an up-to-date and insightful guide to the current state of Japanese society, trade, and commerce.

Ishihara, Shintaro, *The Japan That Can Say No: Why Japan Will be First Among Equals* (Toronto: Touchstone, 1989). Ishihara's book is a controversial and aggressive commentary on Japan's critics and an appeal to the Japanese to take a more assertive economic and political role in the world.

Koren, Leonard, *283 Useful Ideas from Japan* (USA: Chronicle Books, 1988). Japan is famous for its unusual and quirky business ideas—some of which end up as valuable international products. This book describes a range of interesting Japanese products and services.

Lewis, Richard, *When Cultures Collide* (London: Nicholas Brealey Publishing, 1996). This book is a useful guide to working in and communication across different cultures.

McAllinn, G.P., ed., *The Business Guide to Japan* (Singapore: Reed Academic Publishing Asia, 1996). This volume assembles contributions from a number of leading academic commentators on the current state of the Japanese business environment. It provides very interesting and practical technical comments and advice.

Reischauer, Edward, *The Japanese Today: Change and Continuity* (London: Harvard University Press, 1988). Reicschauer's books is one of the classic studies of Japan and has been used to teach several generations of foreigners about the country. While elements have been criticized from time to time, it remains the single best survey of the country.

Rowland, Diane, *Japanese Business Etiquette: A Practical Guide to Success with the Japanese* (New York: Warner, 1993). This is an excellent guide to the inner workings of Japanese business etiquette, with important advice on the details of Japanese social conventions.

Shelley, Rex and Reiko Makiuchi, *Culture Shock! Japan* (Singapore: Times Editions, 1996). This survey provides a very helpful guide to the nuances of Japanese culture and to the difficulties that foreigners face when they attempt to enter this unique society.

Smith, Patrick, *Japan: A Reinterpretation* (New York: Harper Collins, 1997). Smith has provided a very useful overview of Japan's history. This book provides compelling evidence of the connection between Japan's past and present.

Taylor, Jared, *Shadows of the Rising Sun: A Critical View of the Japanese Miracle* (Tokyo: Tuttle, 1993). There have been many critical interpretations of Japan's economic successes, focusing on the social costs and economic tensions that accompanied the Japanese boom. Taylor's account provides some inside insights into the difficulties that followed the country's rapid expansion.

Whitney, Jane, ed., *Doing Business in Japan; An Insider's Guide* (Toronto: Canadian Chamber of Commerce in Japan, 1994). Whitney and her collaborators have offered a useful summary of the options, opportunities, and pitfalls involved with doing business in Japan. While the material is provided from a Canadian perspective, business people from other countries will find it helpful.

Zimmerman, Mark, *How to Do Business with the Japanese* (Tokyo: Tuttle, 1985). Zimmerman's study is one of the classic works on doing business in Japan. While it is now somewhat dated, it provides excellent insights into the interplay of culture and commerce and the difficulties that foreigners have when attempting to set up shop in the country.

Web sites on Business, Economy, and Government

The Internet has emerged as one of the best sources of up-to-date information on business and the economy. (Due to the dynamic nature of the Internet, some web sites stay current longer than others.) The following sites are among the very best locations for Japanese material.

American Chamber of Commerce in Japan—this web-sites connects users to one of the most active foreign business organizations in Japan.
http://www.accj.or.jp/default.asp

Asia Links.com—a very good commercial site that provides access to a great deal of information on contemporary Japan and Asia.
http://www.asia-links.com/japan/

Hyogo Business and Cultural Centre—a useful private site with interesting connections to a variety of commercial, social, artistic. and recreational sources.
http://www.hyogobcc.org/

IBJ Securities Research and Links—a very good private site that offers links to a variety of commercial and business sites. Useful for up-to-date financial information.
http://www.ibjs.co.jp/Kohgin.html/ResrLinkE.html

Japan Business Center—a commercial site providing information on the challenges and opportunities of setting up a business in Japan.
http://www.jbc.gol.com/

Japan External Trade Organization—JETRO is an incredibly helpful government agency that is devoted to assisting with international trade. The web site contains a wealth of useful information and contacts.
http://www.jetro.go.jp/

Japan Institute of Policy Research—a useful connection to an organization that provides general policy research on matters of national importance.
http://www.jipr.org/

Japanese Government and Politics Information—a very general site with excellent links to numerous government and official organizations. http://fuji.stanford.edu/jguide/gov/

Keidanren (Japanese Economic Organization)—the Keidanren is an active research organization that provides a strong business voice on government policies and on the state and direction of the national economy. Japanese politicians pay a great deal of attention to this agency.
http://www.keidanren.or.jp/

Ministry of Finance, Japanese Government—a key source of government financial information.
http://www.mof.go.jp/english/index.htm

Ministry of Foreign Affairs of Japan—an excellent place to find the official Japanese position on major political and international issues.
http://www2.nttca.com:8010/infomofa/index.html

Ministry of Posts and Telecommunications—this Ministry is responsible for telecommunications and the Internet, and thus plays a major role in the development of the digital economy.
http://www.mpt.go.jp/

NikkeiNet Commercial Guide—an excellent guide to Japanese companies and business information.
http://www.nni.nikkei.co.jp/FR/AWG/#japan

NikkeiNet Interactive—a very good (but shortly to become a pay site) source of business and market intelligence.
http://www.nni.nikkei.co.jp/

The Export-Import Bank of Japan—a useful guide to one of the agencies charged with increasing international trade.
http://www.japanexim.go.jp/

The Ministry of International Trade and Industry—MITI is one of the most powerful government agencies in Japan. The web site provides access to some of their central policy statements and programs.
http://www.miti.go.jp/index-e.html

US-Japan Technology Management Center—a useful site that provides insight into American-Japanese initiatives in the fast-growing field of technology and business.
http://fuji.stanford.edu/index.html

World Wide Web Virtual Library for Japan—this academic site is an excellent source for web-based information on all aspects of Japan. It contains links to hundreds of sites.
http://fuji.stanford.edu/jguide/

Internet Guides to Working, Living, and traveling in Japan

Career Strategy Inc.—a commercial job service that helps professionals looking for work in Japan.
http://www.csinc.co.jp/eindex.html

Excite Travel Guide to Japan—useful commercial guide to traveling in Japan.
http://www.city.net/countries/japan/

Gaijin Net—excellent site with information for foreigners living in Japan.
http://www.gaijin-net.com/

Guide to Living in Japan—this location provides detailed information on the technical and social aspects of living in Japan.
http://www.ntt.co.jp/japan/living/lm.html

Intersupport—useful guide for foreigners adjusting to living and working in Japan.
http://www3.hankyu.co.jp/is/is-home.html

Japan Information Network—excellent source of information on the various cities and regions of Japan. This site will help you discover Japan beyond Tokyo.
http://www.jinjapan.org/region/index.html

Japan Times Newspaper—web site of the leading English-language Japanese newspaper. Excellent archive of previous stories.
http://www.japantimes.co.jp/

Japan Travel Updates—helpful information on getting around Japan.
http://www.jnto.go.jp/

The Japanese Professional Job Site—this site seeks to bring applicants and recruiters together.
http://www.jpjs.co.uk/

Tokyo Food Page—excellent diner's guide to the many restaurants of Tokyo.
http://www.twics.com/~robbs/tokyofood.html

Tokyo Q (Weekly Guide to Tokyo Life)—web version of a Tokyo weekly magazine.
http://www.so-net.or.jp/tokyoq/

Tokyo Subway Navigator—search engine that helps you figure out your way around Tokyo by subway.
http://metro.ratp.fr:10001/bin/select/english/japan/tokyo

About the Authors

CARIN HOLROYD is an assistant professor in Japanese business studies at the University of New Brunswick at Saint John. She studied at the University of British Columbia, Chaminade University of Hawaii/Sophia University, and the University of Waikato in New Zealand. Her current research project focuses on Japanese trade and foreign companies' adaptations to the Japanese marketplace.

KEN COATES is professor of history and politics and Dean of Arts at the University of New Brunswick at Saint John. His research interests include Japanese use of the Internet and the development of electronic commerce. Carin and Ken have cowritten *Pacific Partners: The Japanese Presence in Canadian Business, Culture and Society* (Lorimer, 1996).

Index